N Y Life Ins Corp
cover infor Ser
51 Maddisen ave
ny 10, n y

D1267793

THE BOOK NOBODY KNOWS

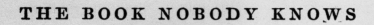

By BRUCE BARTON

THE MAN
NOBODY KNOWS

The Man Nobody Knows is a book different from any other that has been written about Christ. Mr. Barton's interpretation is reverent; it will interest everybody. *The Man Nobody Knows* was written out of sincere conviction. That is evident from the first page to the last.

—*New York Times Book Review.*

The BOOK NOBODY KNOWS

By
BRUCE BARTON

AUTHOR OF
The Man Nobody Knows, Etc.

THE BOBBS-MERRILL COMPANY
PUBLISHERS   INDIANAPOLIS

About a week before the death of Sir Walter
Scott, he said to his son-in-law, Lockhart, "Read
to me from the Book."
"And when I asked him from what book, he said,
'Need you ask? There is but one.'"
—*The Bible in Scots Literature,*
JAMES MOFFATT.

I am indebted to my good friend, Thomas H. Beck, President of P. F. Collier & Son Company, for the title of this little book, and to my father, Reverend William E. Barton, D. D., for very great help in gathering and arranging the material.

BRUCE BARTON.

CONTENTS

I
AN OUTLINE OF HISTORY

QUESTIONS

1. *What is an easy way to remember how many books there are in the Old Testament? In the New Testament?*
   Answered in this chapter.

2. *Who commanded the sun to stand still? Why?*
   Joshua 10:12-13.

3. *Who was the first murderer in the Bible? Whom did he murder? Why?*
   Genesis 4:8-9; I John 3:12.

4. *Who built the ark?*
   Genesis 6:5-22.

5. *What is the origin and meaning of the rainbow?*
   Genesis 9:8-18.

6. *Who was the beautiful woman for whom Jacob served fourteen years?*
   Genesis 29:20-30.

7. *Who was the strongest man in the Bible? The wisest? The longest lived?*
   Judges 14:4-6; I Kings 3:11-14; Genesis 5:27.

8. *What is the origin of the word "shibboleth"?*
   Judges 12:4-6.

9. *Who was Goliath? Who killed him?*
   I Samuel 17:4-11; I Samuel 17:49.

10. *What was Jephthah's vow?*
    Judges 11:30-36.

THE BOOK NOBODY KNOWS

I

AN OUTLINE OF HISTORY

AN INTELLIGENT and talkative lady found herself at dinner seated beside a bishop. Having a social gift, she knew that most men are flattered to be met in conversation on their own grounds, and so she started to talk about the Bible.

"I can't pretend that I read it as much as I should," she confessed, "and really you know parts of it seem to me hopelessly out of date. Yet," she added broadmindedly, "I'll admit that here are some very beautiful passages."

"Yes?" said the Bishop. "For instance?"

"Well, for example, that line about God tempering the wind to the shorn lamb." (On the chance that there may be one or possibly two readers whose knowledge is no more exact than that of this fair lady, let us hasten to remark that "God tempers the wind to the shorn

13

lamb" is in Sterne's *Sentimental Journey,* a book which resembles the Bible about as much as *Robinson Crusoe* resembles the *Encyclopedia Britannica.*)

"And now you must tell me *your* favorite verse," the lady continued brightly.

"It would be hard for me to pick a single verse," the Bishop answered. "But I can give you my favorite passage. It is the one that tells about Eliza crossing the ice."

Not long ago I met a man who wanted to know which of the Old Testament books contains the verse: "Thus saith the Lord, Every tub shall stand upon its own bottom." The answer is that both Jeremiah and Ezekiel give expression to bits of philosophy that resemble this, but not in words that bear any resemblance to it whatever.

It would be easy to multiply such stories. They illustrate a strange phenomenon. Here is a book, or more properly a collection of books, which is beyond comparison the world's best seller. New novels grip the public fancy for a few weeks or months and then disappear, but the Bible stands continuously at the top of the list. Go "somewhere east of Suez," where there "aren't no Ten Commandments," and what do you find? A fine big bookstore in Rangoon, which city you have to visit "on the road to Mandalay," centrally located and up-to-date, with a modern printing office in the rear. American presses are turning out text-books and literature of every sort. And Bibles, cords of Bibles, literally cords of them. Go into the finest hotel in any American city and on the stand at the head of your bed—the last thing to meet your glance at night and the first thing in the morning—is a copy of this same most-circulated book. Nearly every home has at least one copy. Millions of copies are given as birthday, graduation and Christmas gifts. It is a book that everybody buys and concerning which almost everybody is ready to engage in debate at the drop of a hat. Yet how many read it? How many know what it really contains?

It is *worth* knowing. Not all of it, of course. There are long chapters of genealogy which are no more edifying than pages of the telephone directory. There are First and Second Chronicles, which recite the tedious mistakes and sins of kings who were no better than the kings of England and not half so important in their influence on our lives. But when you have passed over such passages and everything else that for popular reading is tiresome or useless, what have you left? These four great treasures:

1. A bird's-eye view of the development of civilization, a sort of Outline of History, as Mr. Wells would say. The story begins with the origin of the earth, just as Wells does, and for the first eleven chapters it deals with the human race as a unit. Coming down to the time when races were grouped and nations arose, it traces the development of a particular people, the Hebrews—their beginnings as nomadic shepherds, their conquest and settlement of a home, and their emergence into national life; their rise to splendor under Kings David and Solomon; their overthrow and captivity, and the reestablishment of their national cult or worship, though with very limited authority in the matter of government, a century later. The recital brings us finally into definite touch with the civilizations of Greece and Rome, the latter being the dominant power throughout the whole period of the New Testament. Considered simply as an historic outline, this is a venture to challenge respect; certainly no one can claim to know history who has not read and understood it.

2. Some of the greatest literature of all ages. Here, to mention only a few, are the greatest of all poems, one of the greatest dramas, one of the finest love-stories, and a collection of proverbs which in varying phraseology have entered into

the common-sense philosophy of nearly every modern nation.

3. The best of all text-books in human nature. William Lyon Phelps is a college professor, as well as an interesting writer and a remarkable human being. When he speaks of education it is fair to assume that he knows what he is talking about. He says: "I thoroughly believe in a university education for both men and women; but I believe a knowledge of the Bible without a college course is more valuable than a college course without the Bible. For in the Bible we have profound thought beautifully expressed; we have the nature of boys and girls, of men and women, more accurately charted than in the work of any modern novelist or playwright. You can learn more about human nature by reading the Bible than by living in New York."

4. Finally, we have the story of the most successful life ever lived on this planet, a life that changed the course of human thought and that still is able, after more than nineteen hundred years, to transform individuals, communities and nations.

Surely it is worth while to know the high spots, at least, of a book that contains all this. Let us start at the beginning with the title page of the common version.

The first line reads, "The Holy Bible." Since the word *biblia* in Latin is plural and means *library,* we know at once that we have here not a single book but a collection of several books.

The second line, "Containing the Old and New Testaments," means obviously that there are two main divisions and that the distinguishing feature is a difference in age, one group of books being more recent than the other.

The third line says, "Translated out of the original tongues," indicating that the Bible was originally published not in English but in more than one other language.

"And with the former translations diligently compared and revised," shows that this translation, which was made under the authority of King James I in 1611, is the successor to several earlier translations.

Turning over the pages we discover that the text is divided into numbered chapters and verses, which seems rather an unusual way to present a book until we learn that these divisions were not made by the original writers but were inserted in 1551 by Mr. Robert Stephens, a pious printer, who believed that more people would read the Bible if he made it easier to read. Several earlier attempts had been made to divide the books into chapters and verses, all

18

of them unsatisfactory. The divisions of Mr. Stephens are far from perfect and, indeed, the story goes that he made them while riding his horse to and fro between his home and the printing office, and that occasionally the horse stumbled and his pencil slipped. There are some glaring mistakes which would seem to lend color to this tale, but Mr. Stephens did remarkable work on the whole, and his general scheme will probably never be discarded.

A single glance is enough to indicate that the Old Testament is much larger than the New— and here is an easy way to remember how many books are in each. The key number is three, which multiplied by itself gives nine. The Old Testament has thirty-nine books. Again multiply three by nine and you have twenty-seven, the number of the books in the New Testament. Once you get that into your mind it is like "thirty days has September"; you can't forget it even if you try.

Cæsar, you remember, divided all Gaul into three parts. Similarly scholars divide the Old Testament into three divisions—the historic books, beginning with Genesis and ending with Esther; the poetic books, beginning with Job and ending with the Song of Songs; and the remainder, which consists of sermons, or, as they are more commonly called, books of prophecy.

Of the historic books the first five have a certain unity which has long caused them to be regarded as one. They are called the Pentateuch, meaning the five-in-one book, and there is a tradition that Moses wrote them all. Whether he did or not we can leave to the scholars to dispute, but there is no doubt that he is the dominating figure in all five books. And what a figure! These are the five:

Genesis—the book of beginnings.

Exodus—the book of going out.

Leviticus—the book for the priests.

Numbers—a sort of amplified census report.

Deuteronomy—a Greek name meaning "second law," or review and digest of the laws.

There are some wonderful things in Leviticus for the student of history. For example, many of the laws of health and sanitation on which we moderns pride ourselves are distinctly set forth here. We think of the disinfection of a house where there has been contagious disease as a comparatively recent development in medical science, but Moses prescribed that the blankets of the sick man should be burned and the house thoroughly purified. Numbers, also, has some high lights, but speaking generally these two

books are less interesting than the other three
and may well be omitted if one is reading to
get the best in the easiest way.

Start in then with the first chapter of Genesis
and you are gripped at once. Here is no pref-
ace, no argument, only a great declaration:

> In the beginning God created the heaven and the
> earth. And the earth was without form, and void;
> and darkness was upon the face of the deep. And
> the Spirit of God moved upon the face of the
> waters. And God said, Let there be light: and
> there was light.

Viewed only as a piece of good writing that
paragraph is superb. What a way to begin a
story! How dignified, how impressive! How
swift and sure the movement! How nobly
superior to the Greek mythologies, and free
from their grossness and puerility!

There is an old anecdote, attributed usually
to Charles A. Dana, about a reporter who protested that a certain news story could not be
compressed into a column. Dana sent him to
the Bible. "Read the first chapter of Genesis,"
he commanded. "You'll find the whole story of
the creation in less than six hundred words." It
is true. The whole story is there in one chapter,
majestic in its simplicity, every line fraught with
meaning and interest.

If you argue that Evolution tells the story very differently, your argument is only partly true. What does Evolution say? That in the beginning there was nothing but nebulous matter; that it gathered itself first into hot shapeless planets, which by revolving grew round; then into land and water; that gradually vegetation appeared, then life in low forms, then higher forms, and finally man. Look back at Genesis and you are surprised perhaps to discover a certain method of progress in its account which is not at all at variance with the best scientific knowledge.

It, too, starts with matter fluid and formless, "without form, and void." But the matter is not wholly inert; the creative Spirit (the scientists say the "First Cause," which means nothing much except that they don't know) is brooding over that vast shapeless egg and incubating something of purpose. The matter is in motion. It separates itself into masses. There is distinction between that which belongs to the earth and that which is of other bodies. Upon the earth the waters gather into oceans, and land is seen in continents.

Then we emerge into biology. Life appears first in low and simple forms. Life in the water and life in the air. Life that creeps and life that

22

flies and life that walks. The higher animals are evolved or created, whichever term suits you better. And last of all, man. His place at the top of the pyramid of creation is the same in both Genesis and geology, the difference being that Genesis compresses into six hundred words what science expands into hundreds of volumes, and Genesis has a reason for man's creation and a goal for his life, while science throws up its hands with the blank admission, "We do not know."

So we have man and woman launched forth upon a brand-new planet. Science locates the beginnings of human life in the fertile and fragrant valley of the Euphrates. Genesis is more specific, naming the beautiful spot the "Garden of Eden," and identifying the first couple as Adam and Eve. Let us take a running look at these two interesting people and the more important of their descendants, for in the Old Testament, as in all other historical records, the history of peoples is principally the lives of a few outstanding individuals.

A lecturer on woman suffrage once challenged her audience with the oratorical question, "Where, I ask you, where would man be to-day if it were not for woman?" To which a rather thick voice from the rear benches answered, "In

the Garden of Eden eating strawberries."
Adam, our first ancestor, does not make a very
brave showing. He and Eve were given the run
of the Garden, with permission to eat any fruit
except that of one particular tree. They ate the
forbidden fruit and when God discovered them
in their transgression Adam took refuge behind
Eve. "The woman whom thou gavest to be with
me," he complained, "she gave me of the tree,
and I did eat." A cowardly excuse which prof-
ited him nothing. For their sin they were cast
out, and the Garden was closed to them. No
longer could they have food without effort.

> Cursed is the ground for thy sake; in sorrow
> shalt thou eat of it all the days of thy life; Thorns
> also and thistles shall it bring forth to thee; . . .
> In the sweat of thy face shalt thou eat bread, till
> thou return unto the ground; for out of it wast
> thou taken: for dust thou art, and unto dust shalt
> thou return.

Eve had two sons, Cain and Abel. As a
shepherd Abel had nothing to do but sit on the
side of a green hill and watch his flocks grow
fat, making money for him the while. Cain was
a farmer, and any one who has ever worked on
a farm understands why farmers in all ages have
been discontented and will realize how Cain felt.
In his jealousy over Abel's easy life and calm

demeanor Cain slew him. "Am I my brother's keeper?" he demanded in surly tones when God made inquiry for Abel. The question has come down through the generations as a text for a million sermons.

Cain seems to have had good stuff in him, regardless of his envious nature and terrible temper; at least his descendants were successful. One of them, Jubal, was the first musician; and another, Tubal-Cain, as the first blacksmith, founded the useful arts. We skip over a number of other interesting characters, noting only that "there were giants in those days," and that men lived to wondrous old age. Adam, in spite of the necessity for hard work, hung on for a matter of nine hundred and thirty years, but the prize for longevity goes to Methusaleh, who established the world's record of nine hundred and sixty-nine years. He passed away in the year of the flood; there is no telling how long he might have lived under a dry régime. Old as these patriarchs were, they did not learn wisdom with their years. In fact their misdemeanors were so flagrant that

> It repented the Lord that he had made man on the earth, and it grieved him at his heart.

There seemed to be no remedy but to wipe

out the whole race and make a fresh start. One man and his family—Noah, his wife and his sons, Shem, Ham and Japheth—were selected for survival, and Noah was instructed to build an ark that would hold them, together with a male and female representative of each species. He was allowed to warn his neighbors, but when in any age has the hopeful human race been willing to face bad news? They jeered at his stories of the coming storm; they stood around the dry-dock where he was working on his ark and passed the same sort of crude jokes with which the folks of a later day greeted Fulton and his *Clermont*. Noah was angry, but he kept at work and had the last laugh. The rain began, and

> every living substance was destroyed which was upon the face of the ground, both man, and cattle, and the creeping things, and the fowl of the heaven; and they were destroyed from the earth: and Noah only remained alive, and they that were with him in the ark.

God has never again indulged in this wholesale effort at reformation, probably because He discovered that the first attempt did so little good. The descendants of Noah lived much shorter lives than the patriarchs, but they were up to pretty much all the bad tricks, as we shall see.

One thing which makes the Bible so interesting and so educational is the fact that it presents its great figures in their entirety—no cloaking of their mistakes, no effort to set them up on pedestals. We see *ourselves* in these pages, with all our passions and frailties, all our hopes and affections, our victories and defeats.

Years passed and grew to centuries, and the great figure of Abraham emerged, a wealthy shepherd having flocks that roamed over so wide an area that he was brought into conflict with rival ranchmen and had to fight for his rights. As a citizen Abraham was open-handed, hospitable and successful in business; and though his treatment of his wife left much to be desired, he had both vision and courage. When God commanded him to leave his country and go into another he "departed as the Lord had spoken unto him" and was rewarded by becoming the father of a mighty people. A sense of humor was one of his assets, a quality not too common in the Bible. When it was promised to him that he and his wife Sarah should have a son

Abraham fell upon his face, and laughed, and said in his heart, Shall a child be born unto him that is

an hundred years old? and shall Sarah, that is
ninety years old, bear?

But Sarah did bear, and they named the boy
Isaac, which means laughter; a name which
ought to have guaranteed him a merry life, but
did not.

Like many sons of great men Isaac lacked the
qualities which make for greatness. He was a
good man but something of a dreamer, who
allowed his father to select a wife for him and
promptly became subject to her will. The story
of the wooing of Rebecca is the first romance
in the Bible, and makes pretty reading. But
Rebecca was a strong-minded woman who knew
what she wanted, and her principal desire was
to supplant her eldest son Esau and put her
second son and favorite, Jacob, in line for Isaac's
property.

Esau, being a hard-working farmer and an
outdoor man, was hairy; Jacob was smooth-
handed, literally and figuratively. Isaac, the
father, had grown old and blind. Rebecca made
a pair of gloves of kid skin for Jacob and sent
him to Isaac with food and a request for the
inheritance.

> And Isaac said unto Jacob, Come near, I pray
> thee, that I may feel thee, my son, whether thou be
> my very son Esau, or not. And Jacob went near

unto Isaac his father; and he felt him [the hairy gloves], and said, The voice is Jacob's voice, but the hands are the hands of Esau. . . . so he blessed him.

Jacob, shrewd and unprincipled, met his match in Laban, who was to become his father-in-law. Laban had two daughters, a homely one named Leah and a beauty, Rachel. Jacob agreed to serve Laban seven years if he might have Rachel for his wife. At the end of the seven years Laban gave him Leah instead and insisted that he serve a second seven-year period for Rachel. Jacob stuck to it, and he and Rachel were finally married and proceeded to repay their loving parent in kind by taking all the best cattle and leaving him sickly ones. With this fine moral start they set up house-keeping, and Jacob lost no time in becoming the father of twelve sons, of whom the next to the youngest, Joseph, is the second important figure after the flood.

The oldest of the twelve brothers was Reuben, to whom Jacob on his death-bed said signif-icantly, "unstable as water, thou shalt not excel." He would have liked to protect Joseph from the envious hatred of the others, who saw all too clearly Jacob's favoritism for him, but Reuben was too weak to accomplish anything.

The hatred of the others cast Joseph into a deep pit. It was their first intention to kill him, but at the suggestion of Reuben, who wanted to save Joseph's life, and could plan no other way, he was lifted out and sold to a passing caravan and taken to Egypt.

A fine parade of human attributes now marches before us—Potiphar, captain in the service of Pharaoh, who took a liking to Joseph and made him an overseer; Mrs. Potiphar, who fell in love with the bright youngster and, when out of his loyalty to her husband, Joseph refused her advances, caused him to be cast into prison; the royal butler, whose release Joseph secured by interpreting a dream, and who promised in turn to get Joseph out of jail, but success quickly banishes the memory of old-time friends.

> Yet did not the chief butler remember Joseph, but forgat him.

Presently, however, Joseph secured his own release, having been able to interpret a dream for Pharaoh himself. Pharaoh had seen in his dream seven fat cattle and seven lean cattle, and behold the seven lean cattle ate up the seven fat ones. What could it mean? "It means," said Joseph, "that we are going to have seven good business years and then seven very bad ones; and we better get ready for the bad ones right away." Thus Joseph made the first Babson chart, showing that the area of financial inflation precedes that of depression and is of equal size and density. Babson has publicly admitted that he got the idea from Joseph, and it has made him a fortune, even as it caused Joseph to be promoted in the public service until he was second only to the king. Through Joseph's foresight and organizing ability the Egyptians stored up food in the seven fat years and came through the lean years with flying colors.

Joseph was big in nature as well as in ability. He sent for his father and brethren, forgave them, got them good jobs in the public service and settled them in luxury in his adopted country. Thus things went swimmingly for the children of Israel until Joseph died, after which calamity descended. The Pharaoh who had been so friendly also died and "there arose a new king in Egypt which knew not Joseph." Envy and jealousy of these smart fellows were rampant; there was a universal demand that they should be evicted from the rich jobs and fat concessions. They not only were evicted but they were thrust down to the very bottom of the social ladder. Having been rulers, they were made slaves, and their bitter servitude prepared the way for the next great figure—one of the mighty men of all history—Moses, law-giver, organizer, builder of a nation.

One of the wicked decrees of Pharaoh was that every son who was born to the Hebrews should be cast into the river. The mother of Moses managed to hide her baby for three months, and then, unable to secrete him any longer, she made a little cradle and set him afloat in the River Nile near the spot where the daughter of Pharaoh and her maidens came down to bathe. Pharaoh's daughter took compassion on the pitiful little voyager, carried him with her to the palace and reared him as her own. She gave him his name, Moses, which means "draw-out"; "because," she said, "I drew him out of the water." The boy grew up with all the educational advantages which the palace could give, but his heart was true to his people. He had hardly reached his full stature of manhood when he ran afoul of an Egyptian taskmaster who was abusing a poor Hebrew workman. Moses slew the man and hid his body, and formed then and there the determination to set the Hebrews free.

With his brother Aaron, who was a good talker, which Moses was not, he carried on extended negotiations with Pharaoh, enforcing his arguments by a series of ten plagues that descended upon the Egyptians. In the end he was allowed to lead the Hebrews forth into the wilderness, but Pharaoh changed his mind at the last moment and gave pursuit. It was a fatal decision. The Red Sea, which had separated to let the Hebrews pass through, closed up on Pharaoh and his army and drowned them every one. So Moses was launched on his career as leader of a grumbling, short-sighted and dis-contented lot of ex-slaves, who continually annoyed him with their complaint that they would rather be back in their slavery than wandering free in the wilderness.

Moses was not only a leader but an executive as well, thanks partly to his father-in-law Jethro. That wise old gentleman, visiting him in the wilderness on a day when he was holding court, saw the tremendous pressure which was on him in his combined capacity of ruler and judge, and protested:

> Thou wilt surely wear away, both thou, and this people that is with thee: for this thing is too heavy for thee: thou art not able to perform it thyself alone.

Acting on the old man's sound advice, Moses associated certain other upright men with him

as judges, and thus it came about that the
people were provided not only with a law—
through the Ten Commandments and the comprehensive Mosaic Code—but with a judiciary
as well.

The Ten Commandments are, of course, the
outstanding monument to Moses' wisdom and
influence. Read them over. How direct; how
simple; how free from superfluous or trivial in-
junctions. They drive straight at the heart of
human and divine relationships, and are the
corner-stone upon which the nations have erected
their legal and ethical codes. But they are not
the only survival of Moses' leadership. The
long, carefully molded Mosaic Law is hardly
less remarkable. It embraces both a civil and
a criminal code and foreshadowed by centuries
not only our modern jurisprudence but much of
our modern health regulation and medical practise.

On the civil side there is protection of property
and reputation. There are exemption laws providing that the outer garment of a poor man,
given by him in pawn, shall be returned to him
at night; laws providing that the land that has
been mortgaged and forfeited shall be restored
to the family at the end of a period of years;
laws punishing libel and protecting the good

name of man and woman. There are laws providing that a poor man's wages are not to be retained to his injury. On the other hand, judges are warned not to favor a poor man but to render equal justice. Taxes were light and levied in proportion to a man's property, but there was one tax concerning which it was provided that the rich should not be permitted to pay more nor the poor allowed to pay less. It was a small tax, but it represented manhood and self-respect and equality before the law.

Some of the regulations went far beyond ordinary legal limits and prescribed the conduct of a gentleman:

> Thou shalt not curse the deaf, nor put a stumblingblock before the blind, but shalt fear thy God: I am the Lord. . . .
>
> Thou shalt not go up and down as a talebearer. . . .
>
> Thou shalt not hate thy brother in thine heart. . . .
>
> Thou shalt rise up before the hoary head, and honour the face of the old man, and fear thy God; I am the Lord.
>
> And if a stranger sojourn with thee in your land, ye shall not vex him.
>
> But the stranger that dwelleth with you shall be unto you as one born among you, and thou shalt love him as thyself.

The criminal code was severe and swift, but

inflexibly just. Life was protected and murder punished with death. Even accidental homicide did not go without penalty to him by whose carelessness it occurred, but he was not condemned to death. "An eye for an eye and a tooth for a tooth" sounds severe in these days of sentimental talk about "crime a disease," but it made a law-abiding people, careful of one another's rights.

The sanitary code was extended, minute and enforced with strict penalties. Can you imagine the feat of bringing a horde of escaped slaves across a wilderness without losing them by dysentery, typhoid fever or hook-worm? It was made possible by a simple but powerfully effective system of sewage disposal. That priests and rabbis should have personal supervision of slaughter-houses may seem at first sight like a strange mingling of the spiritual functions with the material; but it preserved the nation from scrofula and other blood disorders, as the isolation of communicable diseases and the strict disinfection under priestly supervision prevented the spread of plagues. Most important of all, the laws of Moses were of such a nature as to minimize the social evil. The healthy sex life of the Jews of ancient times is one of the chief reasons for their amazing racial continuity.

The distance from Egypt to the Promised

Land is no longer than the trip from New York to Buffalo. Moses might easily have led his people over the route in a few weeks, instead of which the wanderings occupied forty years. Guided by divine wisdom, he saw the necessity for a long period of isolated discipline. They were slaves when he started with them; they were an organized self-governing nation when, at length, he climbed to the pinnacle of Mount Pisgah and looked across into the Promised Land, which he was permitted to see but not to enter.

> So Moses, the servant of the Lord, died there in the land of Moab, according to the word of the Lord.
> And he [the Lord] buried him in a valley in the land of Moab, over against Beth-peor; but no man knoweth of his sepulchre unto this day.

How well he had done his work was immediately apparent. Joshua, whom he had chosen to succeed him, took hold without a hitch and completed the journey into Canaan. He, too, was a man of vision. As a young man, he had been sent by Moses with nine others to spy out the Promised Land. Eight of the ten came back with a faint-hearted report.

> It is a land that eateth up the inhabitants there-

of; and all the people that we saw in it are men of a great stature.

And there we saw the giants, the sons of Anak, which come of the giants: and we were in our own sight as grasshoppers, and so we were in their sight.

Thus you can always get a majority vote to do nothing, to take no chances. But there was a minority report. Joshua and Caleb, without minimizing the difficulties, protested stoutly that the land was fertile and worth fighting for. They brought back samples of fruit to prove their contention, and the people took courage from them and moved on.

Joshua was a soldier and was much needed for the work which Moses had left to be done. He led his people across the Jordan, engineered the successful attack upon Jericho, the walled city of the unfortunate people who happened to be in possession of the Promised Land, and conducted a triumphal campaign which was about as savage as any war could be. Finally, his work completed, he called his people together for a farewell address of great dignity and power. "Behold, this day I am going the way of all the earth," he told them; and with that he laid aside his arms and died.

Comes now a picturesque succession of

leaders, called Judges, with whom we can tarry only a moment in this rapid survey. There was a woman, Deborah, among them, whose stirring battle-hymn is one of the first recorded poems. There was a keen fighter named Gideon, a shrewd strategist, who equipped his slender force of three hundred men with chariot lights and trumpets and attacked at night. The enemy, roused from complacent slumber, hearing the din of trumpets and seeing the lights charging down upon them from every hillside, imagined that a host of chariots was attacking, and took to flight. So Gideon won a bloodless victory.

Some of the judges made their way up from the lower ranks, for national necessity knows no respect for pedigree. Of these Abimelech was the son of a housemaid, and Jephthah the son of a harlot. There was Samson, the strong man, who had been promised that his strength should remain with him as long as he did not cut his hair. A good-natured, easy-going fellow he was, fond of athletic sports and overfond of women. Delilah wormed his secret from him, cut off his hair while he slept and delivered him to the Philistines, who put out his eyes and amused themselves with his labors as a slave.

In their triumph they did not notice that his hair was growing every day, and when at a great feast they sent for him to make sport, he bribed his guide to let him stand between the pillars of the temple. With one mighty heave he thrust them apart burying himself and his enemies in a common grave.

> So the dead which he slew at his death were more than they which he slew in his life.

Finally there was Samuel, stern, uncompromising, incorruptible. He was not a particularly lovable character, and his powerful one-man rule does not seem to have left a place for any associates. At least the people saw no one capable of carrying on in his place, and reminded him brutally that his own sons were failures.

> Behold, thou art old, and thy sons walk not in thy ways; now make us a king to judge us like all the nations.

Angrily Samuel agreed, but not without a warning. Their king would be tyrannical, he told them; they would repent their demand. None the less he acceded to it, and searching through the tribes he found a clean-cut young man named Saul who stood head and shoulders above all the rest. Him he selected and anointed as Israel's first king.

"God save the king," shouted the people hap-

pily—the first time in history that the cry had
been raised—and indeed it looked as though
their happiness were justified. They had a
brave and handsome monarch whose modesty
was as striking as his courage. What now could
stop them from complete success? But Saul's
career is one of the great tragedies. He might
have been the George Washington of his people,
but he could not stand prosperity, and so little
permanent imprint did he leave that the writer
of Hebrews, in enumerating the great characters
of the nation, does not even mention his name.
He was modest and likable, but he was a prey
to sullen moods and the slave of jealousy. He
was jealous of Jonathan, his son, and would
have slain him but for the determined protest
of the people. Most of all was he jealous of
David, who, when the armies of Israel were
standing in helpless terror before the giant
leader of the Philistines, Goliath, took his shepherd's sling, picked up a smooth stone from the
brook and planted it squarely in the giant's fore-
head. For this victory, and the acclaim that
followed it, Saul never forgave him.

Saul was not without military genius. He led
his people more than once to victory. Throughout his career fighting was constant, with the
Amalekites, the Philistines and other hostile

tribes, and sometimes one side won and sometimes the other. But much of the energy and time that ought to have gone into the nation's battles was spent in the vain effort to destroy David; and the net result of Saul's reign was little. "To-morrow," said the ghost of Samuel, appearing grimly before him, "to-morrow shalt thou and thy sons be with me." Saul marched into battle on the morrow knowing that his fate was sealed; and when the final moment of defeat arrived he called upon his sword bearer to run him through, preferring to die like a man rather than be the captive of his enemies.

And David reigned in his stead.

If you are thrilled by Napoleon, the penniless young lieutenant leaping to the throne of an empire; if your imagination is warmed by the rise of the gaunt, homely, country boy Lincoln to the White House, then there is a real treat for you in David. What a romantic story of success! The simple shepherd lad, tending his sheep and playing his lute, receives a sudden summons home. Saul, the King, who is passionately fond of music, has sent out a call for a musician. The boy goes to court and by his modesty and quick intelligence becomes a favorite. The blustering Goliath affords his courage a golden opportunity; in a single hour he wins the gratitude of the nation and with it the jealous hatred of the king. Jonathan, the handsome crown prince, loves him, and between the two boys there springs up one of the sublime friendships of history. Compelled to flee the court, a rebel not by his own wish but because of the insane envy of Saul, he lives for years by his wits, surrounded by the rag-tag and bob-tail of insurgency.

> And every one that was in distress, and every one that was in debt, and every one that was discontented, gathered themselves unto him; and he became a captain over them: and there were with him about four hundred men.

At length Saul dies and David ascends the throne. With firm hand and statesman-like vision he enforces order within the kingdom and respect without. So successful are his campaigns that he is able to establish a garrison in far-off Damascus and levy tribute on the Syrians, while Hyram, the powerful king of Tyre, is glad to claim him as an ally and a friend. He is one of the realest characters in all literature. You can see his sturdy body and strong but kindly face; you hear his tones and feel his presence, for there is no attempt to make him anything more than human. In fact his sin—the great blot on his kingly career—is set forth in complete detail. It is one of the famous illicit love-stories and has been the theme of countless poems and plays.

Walking one afternoon upon the roof of his palace David saw a beautiful woman in her bath. It was love at first sight. He sent immediately to inquire her name, and though it was told him that she was the wife of Uriah the Hittite, he took her into his harem. The act was made more heinous by the fact that Uriah was away, fighting his king's battles at the front. After a period the girl, Bathsheba, brought David the uncomfortable news that she was with child. Then came the act of villainy. David conferred with Joab, his general, and arranged that Uriah should be sent into the very foremost rank at the next battle. Loyally the brave soldier fulfilled his orders and, as had been expected and hoped by the king, he was reported among the casualties. Bathsheba became the favorite of the palace and bore a famous son, Solomon, for whom she secured the succession through her influence over David.

It is not a pretty story, and the prophet Nathan, a rugged old preacher who feared nothing, did not allow the king to forget his sin. Until his dying day David was conscience-stricken. We are quite sure that many of the Psalms which are attributed to him must have been written by others, but we know that he did write this one, a bitter cry of repentance:

> Have mercy upon me, O God, according to thy loving kindness;
> According unto the multitude of thy tender mercies blot out my transgressions. . . .
> Thou desirest not sacrifice; else would I give it; thou delightest not in burnt offering.
> The sacrifices of God are a broken spirit; a broken and a contrite heart, O God, thou wilt not despise.

We know also that the great shepherd psalm was David's, composed probably during the brief insurrection of his son Absalom, when the king was forced to abandon the capital city and flee like a hunted thing in the wilderness:

> The Lord is my shepherd; I shall not want.
> He maketh me to lie down in green pastures: he leadeth me beside the still waters.
> He restoreth my soul; he leadeth me in the paths of righteousness for his name's sake.
> Yea, though I walk through the valley of the shadow of death, I will fear no evil; for thou art with me; thy rod and thy staff they comfort me.
> Thou preparest a table before me in the presence of mine enemies; thou anointest my head with oil; my cup runneth over.

> Surely goodness and mercy shall follow me all
> the days of my life: and I will dwell in the house
> of the Lord for ever.

If David had done nothing more than compose these two poems he would have established
his right to immortality. But he was one of the
great statesmen-kings, lifting his people up to
their high point of national independence and
self-respect. His reign is the climax in this outline of history. Through his leadership and that
of his great predecessors the children of Abraham, who started as wandering shepherds and
passed through the purifying fire of Egyptian
slavery and the harsh schooling of the wilderness,
achieved at last a sense of racial solidarity which
has persisted through the ages.

II
PROVERBS, POEMS AND PROPHETS

QUESTIONS

1. Who was the most patient man that ever lived? Was he?
   Answered in this chapter.

2. Who wrote "The Lord is my shepherd, I shall not want"?
   Psalm 23.

3. What chapter in the Bible discusses good women and bad women and was written by a woman?
   Proverbs 31.

4. Why is a cab driver sometimes called a Jehu?
   II Kings 9:16-20.

5. What beautiful woman said, "Whither thou goest, I will go."
   Ruth 1:16.

6. What prophet was taken up to heaven in a chariot of fire?
   II Kings 2:9-12.

7. What prophet spent three days and nights in the belly of a big fish?
   Jonah 1:17.

8. Who said, "Whoso findeth a wife findeth a good thing, and obtaineth favour of the Lord"?
   Proverbs 18:22.

9. What famous monarch was dramatically warned in the midst of a banquet by "the handwriting on the wall"?
   Daniel 5:1-6.

10. What man in the Bible said he had "escaped with the skin of his teeth"?
    Job 19:20.

II

PROVERBS, POEMS AND PROPHETS

TEN fairly representative people were asked, "What do you know about Solomon?" Four of the ten answered, "Nothing." Other answers were: He had two thousand wives; he was the husband of the Queen of Sheba; he built Solomon's Temple; he was the wisest man that ever lived.

The statistics regarding Solomon's marriages as given in the Book of Kings are "seven hundred wives, princesses, and three hundred concubines." The Queen of Sheba was not officially among this distinguished company. A monarch in her own right, she was so impressed by the stories of Solomon's splendor and wisdom that she made a long journey to visit him and after a series of receptions and banquets returned to her home. The present kings of Abyssinia claim their descent from Solomon and this queen. If they are justified in their proud boast her visit was not wholly Platonic. It may have been true of her, as she said of Solomon that "the half has not been told." All that we know certainly is that she never appears in the Bible again.

Solomon did build the temple and it remained the pride and glory of Jerusalem until the destruction of the city by the Babylonians in 586 B. C. But the most enduring monuments left by this great ruler were not in stone or bronze, but in words—The Proverbs, a rich mine of wisdom wherein every nugget is solid gold. One can only marvel after reading them how a man so wise in other ways could have been so unwise about women.

He made a fine start as king. The Lord appeared one night in a dream, asking him to name his heart's desire, and Solomon answered:

> Thou hast made thy servant king instead of David my father: and I am but a little child: I know not how to go out or come in. . . .
> Give therefore thy servant an understanding heart to judge thy people, that I may discern between good and bad: for who is able to judge this thy so great a people?

To which the Lord replied:

> Because this was in thine heart, and thou hast not asked riches, wealth, or honour, nor the life of thine enemies, neither yet hast asked long life; but hast asked wisdom and knowledge for thyself, that

thou mayest judge my people, over whom I have made thee king:

Wisdom and knowledge is granted unto thee; and I will give thee riches, and wealth, and honour, such as none of the kings have had that have been before thee, neither shall any after thee have the like.

Without this wise choice on the part of Solomon we probably never should have had the Proverbs; but something more than inspired knowledge went into them. They bear evidence of comprehensive experience with every phase of human nature and conduct. Some of them, as might be imagined from Solomon's own record, contain warnings against the unrighteous woman.

For she sitteth at the door of her house, on a seat in the high places of the city,

To call passengers who go right on their ways:

Whoso is simple, let him turn in hither: and as for him that wanteth understanding, she saith to him,

Stolen waters are sweet, and bread eaten in secret is pleasant.

But he knoweth not that the dead are there; and that her guests are in the depths of hell.

Most of the Proverbs could hardly be called religious. They are the shrewd guide-posts to worldly wisdom, by which a man may make his way through life with most profit to himself and least discomfort to other people:

> The fear of the Lord is the beginning of knowledge: but fools despise wisdom and instruction.
> Reprove not a scorner, lest he hate thee: rebuke a wise man, and he will love thee.
> As vinegar to the teeth, and as smoke to the eyes, so is the sluggard to them that send him.
> A false balance is abomination to the Lord: but a just weight is his delight.
> He that is surety for a stranger shall smart for it; and he that hateth suretyship is sure.
> As a jewel of gold in a swine's snout, so is a fair woman which is without discretion.
> He that keepeth his mouth keepeth his life: but he that openeth wide his lips shall have destruction.
> The simple believeth every word: but the prudent man looketh well to his going.
> In all labour there is profit: but the talk of the lips tendeth only to penury.
> The eyes of the Lord are in every place, beholding the evil and the good.
> Better is a dinner of herbs where love is, than a stalled ox and hatred therewith.
> He that is greedy of gain troubleth his own house.
> He that is slow to anger is better than the mighty; and he that ruleth his spirit than he that taketh a city.

Many of the phrases and sentences have entered into our common talk. Everybody knows them, but not everybody knows where they originated.

> Go to the ant thou sluggard; consider her ways, and be wise.
>
> Hope deferred maketh the heart sick.
>
> A soft answer turneth away wrath; but grievous words stir up anger.
>
> It is naught, it is naught, saith the buyer; but when he is gone his way, then he boasteth.
>
> Where there is no vision, the people perish.
>
> He that spareth his rod hateth his son.
>
> A man that hath friends must shew himself friendly.
>
> Wine is a mocker, strong drink is raging; and whosoever is deceived thereby is not wise.
>
> A good name is rather to be chosen than great riches.

Some of the wisest and most memorable observations are set forth in poetic guise, which adds to their impressiveness:

> There be three things which are too wonderful for me, yea, four which I know not:
>
> The way of an eagle in the air; the way of a serpent upon a rock; the way of a ship in the midst of the sea; and the way of a man with a maid.

> For three things the earth is disquieted, and for four which it cannot bear:
>
> For a servant when he reigneth; and a fool when he is filled with meat;

For an odious woman when she is married; and an handmaid that is heir to her mistress.

There be four things which are little upon the earth, but they are exceeding wise:
The ants are a people not strong, yet they prepare their meat in the summer;
The conies are but a feeble folk, yet make they their houses in the rocks;
The locusts have no king, yet go they forth all of them by bands;
The spider taketh hold with her hands, and is in kings' palaces.

These latter selections are not Solomon's, but come from a man named Agur, the son of Jakeh, about whom we know nothing. Another group of sayings is given under the heading, "These also are the sayings of the wise"; and the last chapter of Proverbs is the work of an anonymous writer, presumably a woman, and possibly Bathsheba, that remarkable lady who deserted Uriah the Hittite to become the favorite wife of Israel's greatest king and mother of the wisest.

There are two other Old Testament books which come to mind in connection with Solomon. The first is the "Song of Songs" which, as the first verse says, "is Solomon's," but whether this means by Solomon or concerning Solomon is a question. It is a poem about a young girl who lived in the northern hills. Solomon saw her on his travels and wanted her for his harem, but her heart was true to her shepherd lover. When the ladies of the court praised Solomon to her and demanded, "What is thy lover more than any other?" she answered stoutly, "My beloved is mine, and I am his."

She was carried off to Jerusalem, but she slept fitfully. "I slept but my soul was awake," she said. In her dreams she found herself wandering all about the streets of a strange city, looking for her lover. Finally her loyalty was rewarded. Solomon would not hold her against the hunger of her heart and returned her to her Galilean swain.

This is the story, somewhat involved in the telling but clear enough to any one who will take time to puzzle it out. When you read the italic type at the head of each chapter, however, what do you discover? That this old-fashioned love song is *"an allegory of Christ and the church"!* Nothing could be more absurd. The "Song" is not a religious book in any sense; the name of God does not once occur in it. Its theme is the triumph of virtuous love over all the riches that a king can offer. Simply that and nothing more. When you see how diligently certain annotaters have worked to squeeze all the life and humanity out of the Bible you wonder how the Book has lasted so long. Its vitality, in spite of the bad offices of its friends, is the most powerful argument for its inspiration.

Ecclesiastes is the other book commonly attributed to Solomon because the first verse reads:

> The words of the Preacher, the son of David, king in Jerusalem.

Modern scholars seem to think that some obscure writer of a much later date wrote the book and that the resplendent Solomon gets the credit—a quite plausible conjecture. It is too bad we can not be sure about the authorship, for the writer, whoever he was, left us one of the great masterpieces. Frederick the Great called it the "book for kings," and insisted that every monarch ought to read it regularly. Whenever some one recommends that you buy a current novel which claims to be ultra-modern in its cynical appraisal of life, save your two dollars and take down your Bible and read Ecclesiastes again. You will find in it everything that the Greenwich Villagers have ever said, and much better said than they ever thought of saying it.

It is the book of an old man, who had sought pleasure in every conceivable form but had nowhere found satisfaction.

> Vanity of vanities; all is vanity.

What profit hath a man of all his labor which he taketh under the sun?

One generation passeth away, and another generation cometh: but the earth abideth forever.

The sun also ariseth, and the sun goeth down, and hasteth to his place where he arose. . . .

All the rivers run into the sea; yet the sea is not full; unto the place from whence the rivers come, thither they return again.

All things are full of labour; man cannot utter it; the eye is not satisfied with seeing, nor the ear filled with hearing.

The thing that hath been, it is that which shall be; and that which is done is that which shall be done: and there is no new thing under the sun.

Being in a position of power, and with educational opportunities beyond those of other men, the writer set forth to make himself the wisest of all. But

I perceived that this also is vexation of spirit. For in much wisdom is much grief; and he that increaseth knowledge increaseth sorrow.

He tried to find satisfaction in mirth and wine, and again in achievement—the building of palaces and gardens, the accumulation of property, gold and silver, servants.

Then I looked on all the works that my hands had wrought, and on the labour that I had laboured to do: and, behold, all was vanity and vexation of spirit, and there was no profit under the sun.

So, disillusioned and old, he continues for eleven gloomy chapters, and then suddenly there comes a change in the tempo. He has found the answer, the one thing that gives satisfaction, the one safeguard against a lifetime of fruitless searching and reiterated disappointments.

> Remember now thy Creator in the days of thy youth, while the evil days come not, nor the years draw nigh, when thou shalt say, I have no pleasure in them.

There are scholars who say that this majestic twelfth chapter of Ecclesiastes does not jibe with the other eleven and must have been added by a later hand. True, perhaps, but improbable. It makes a grand conclusion to a very wonderful book, and it belongs just where it is.

From the deep shadows of Ecclesiastes you turn with a sense of relief to the Psalms, filled with the grandeur of the mountains, the fragrance of spring air, the vast stretches of the firmament and the joy of the Lord. To be sure, there are other notes, for the Psalms are a complete emotional record of human life. In them are love, hope, despair, the bitterest of sorrow, the most exultant delight, sweet affection and deep hatred, confession of sin and joy in forgiveness. But the major note is optimistic and believing.

David wrote many of the earlier psalms, and there are some that grew out of his personal experience; but no one man makes a hymn book. Some psalms were written hundreds of years after his death. The man who wrote

> By the rivers of Babylon, there we sat down, yea, we wept, when we remembered Zion. We hanged our harps upon the willows in the midst thereof,

that man gave a page of vivid autobiography that dates itself five hundred years after David. When another singer wrote:

> O God, the heathen are come into thine inheritance; thy holy temple have they defiled; they have laid Jerusalem on heaps. The dead bodies of thy servants have they given to be meat unto the fowls of the heaven,

thus telling of a time when Jerusalem was captured in a bloody battle followed by a massacre, and the temple was defiled but not destroyed, we know that the psalm was written in the times of the Maccabees. It may be that a thousand years separates the oldest of these songs from the latest.

Of the whole, a hundred and fifty songs, which are best worth knowing? First of all the twenty-third, of course. Nearly every child learns it; every child should. If, in addition to this, you would like to pick three others as a part of your children's education, you will be pretty safe if you follow the number nine—the nineteenth; the ninetieth and the ninety-first.

Moses is credited with the ninetieth—the noble chant of an old man, who, seeing his own generation disappear and a new generation rise up to take its place, nevertheless faces the future with serene trust.

> Lord, thou hast been our dwelling place in all generations.
> Before the mountains were brought forth, or ever thou hadst formed the earth and the world, even from everlasting to everlasting, thou art God. . . .
> A thousand years in thy sight are but as yesterday when it is past, and as a watch in the night . . .
> So teach us to number our days, that we may apply our hearts unto wisdom.

The nineteenth acclaims the firmament and the moral law:

> The heavens declare the glory of God; and the firmament showeth his handiwork.

Day unto day uttereth speech, and night unto night sheweth knowledge.

The ninety-first is a majestic confession of faith.

He that dwelleth in the secret place of the most High shall abide under the shadow of the Almighty.

I will say of the Lord, He is my refuge and my fortress; my God; in him will I trust.

Surely he shall deliver thee from the snare of the fowler, and from the noisome pestilence.

There is one other Psalm, a very short one, which in my boyhood was always read aloud at the beginning or completion of a journey. It is a grand hymn of trust for going away and praise for returning safely home, and since it is short we can quote it in full:

I will lift up mine eyes unto the hills, from whence cometh my help.

My help cometh from the Lord, which made heaven and earth.

He will not suffer thy foot to be moved: he that keepeth thee will not slumber.

Behold he that keepeth Israel will neither slumber nor sleep.

The Lord is thy keeper; the Lord is thy shade upon thy right hand.

The sun shall not smite thee by day, nor the moon by night.

The Lord shall preserve thee from all evil; he shall preserve thy soul.

> The Lord shall preserve thy going out and thy coming in from this time forth, and even for evermore.

If the human race lasts for a million years and produces ten million poets, there will not be a grander hymn of faith than those eight verses of the hundred and twenty-first Psalm.

"Why do you call the Psalms poetry?" somebody asks. "They don't rhyme." Hebrew poetry does not consist of rhyme nor meter, but in balance of thought, a parallelism. One line says a thing and the next repeats it with slight and skilful variation.

> In the way of righteousness is life; and in the pathway thereof is no death.

Or the second line is an adversative clause:

> Wealth gotten by vanity shall be diminished: but he that gathereth by labour shall have increase.

Thus the balance and rhythm are not in the words but in the thought. Having in mind this distinctive characteristic, it is easier to understand why the Book of Job is called sometimes "the greatest poem" and sometimes "the greatest of all dramas."

Everybody knows Job, "the most patient man

62

who ever lived"—a bit of knowledge based on
the remark in the New Testament: "Ye have
heard of the patience of Job." As a matter of
fact, Job was about as impatient as a man could
possibly be, and properly so perhaps, for he was
the victim of trials quite undeserved. The word
"patience" as the New Testament writer uses
it does not denote the moral quality of submis-
sion with cheerfulness to a hard experience, but
mere endurance—"You have heard how much
Job endured, and know that in the end he had
better fortune," that seems to be about what the
writer means.

Job was a rich farmer, cattle owner and public-
spirited citizen, who headed all subscription lists
and had the satisfaction of seeing his enterprises
succeed and his children grow up with good
promise. Suddenly calamity descends upon
him. He does not know it, but Satan has made
a bargain with God to try his soul. The out-
come of the trial is to determine whether Job, or
any other man, is righteous merely for the love
of righteousness or whether he must be bribed
to righteousness by prosperity and the promise
of heaven.

Job's crops are destroyed, his barns burned,
his children taken sick, and he himself breaks out
all over with horrid boils. In this condition he

is visited by a group of three friends—professional moralists and Pollyannas—and between them and him the dramatic debate ensues. They tell him just where he has been wrong and urge him to confess his sins to God and beg forgiveness. He responds sarcastically,

> No doubt but ye are the people and wisdom shall die with you.

He denies that he has sinned and refuses to tell God that he has because it would be a lie; and he won't lie even to be relieved from all his misfortunes.

His conversation is far from meek, but you can't fail to admire his indomitable courage. In the end it triumphs. God says to him in effect: "Job, you have talked a good deal of nonsense, and you have been very impatient, but you have helped me to win out in my contest with Satan. He said that nobody on earth loves goodness for its own sake, and I told him that you do. He said I was wrong, but you have proved me right. I am proud of you, and I was never so proud as when you protested that you would not lie even to please me."

It is a grand book. It does not furnish any answer to the perplexing problem of suffering. It does not explain why a good man, Job or any

other, should have sorrow visited upon him in a
world which is supposed to be under the control
of a loving God. What it does proclaim is that
God has staked His reputation on His ability
to produce human beings who can stand anything that fate or fortune may bring; men who
will be good without a bribe. It insists that in
this trial of creative strength and moral goodness
God is winning out.

"Every man has his price," says the cynic;
but Job did not have his price. He was stripped
of his possessions, he lost his health, he had a
fool for a wife, and his friends were no comfort
to him. But his head though bloody was un-
bowed. "Even if God does not reward me, and
treats me like a wicked man; even if He has
made a mistake about me, or forgotten me, or
just naturally has it in for me, nevertheless I
stand on my record. I am glad I fed the
hungry and helped people when I could. I
have nothing to repent, and I refuse to lie and
say that I have. *The words of Job are ended.*"
It is a brave speech of a brave man, and small
wonder that God responded to it, restored him
his property, blessed his sons and daughters, and
allowed him to live in prosperity for a hundred
and forty years.

So Job died, being old and full of days.

So much for the poetry of the Old Testament, and the drama.

To pick up our historical outline where we left it at the end of the last chapter, we must go back to King Solomon, who has built his temple and palaces, written his Proverbs, and grown old, his heart being "turned away" by his harem. With a thousand mothers to look after them the children of a king ought to be properly brought up, but the net results in the Solomon household were not so good. His heir, Rehoboam, was a typical rich man's son, soft, conceited, sure of his own opinion and contemptuous of advice. As soon as it was known that "Solomon slept with his fathers," a rough and ready soldier named Jeroboam organized an insurrection, demanding that King Rehoboam lower the taxes and conduct himself in a less arbitrary fashion than had his father.

The old men who had been Solomon's counselors urged Rehoboam to compromise, but the hot-headed young courtiers were all for the Big Stick, and Rehoboam sided with them.

And the king answered the people roughly, and forsook the old men's counsel that they gave him; And spake to them after the counsel of the

young men, saying, My father made your yoke
heavy, and I will add to your yoke; my father
also chastised you with whips, but I will chastise
you with scorpions.

This made it all very easy for Jeroboam, who
promptly persuaded the ten southern tribes to
separate and elect him their king. Rehoboam
kept only Judah and the little tribe of Benjamin.

And there was war between Rehoboam and Jeroboam all their days.

The beginning of the end of the Jewish nation.
All of this took place around 1000 B. C.,
which is a useful date to remember in connection
with David and Solomon. From the death of
Solomon until 586 B. C., when Jerusalem was
destroyed by the Babylonians, the history of the
two little kingdoms is a sad tale of intrigue, sin-
fulness, bad management and steady decline.
Sometimes the kingdoms fought and sometimes
they were allies. In periods of peace the crown
prince of one kingdom was usually named after
the reigning monarch of the other, so that the
record in the Book of Kings is confusing enough
to the average reader. You get the gist of it
in verses like these:

In the thirty and first year of Asa king of

Judah [the smaller kingdom] began Omri to reign
over Israel [the larger] . . .

But Omri wrought evil in the eyes of the Lord
and did worse than all that were before him. . . .

Omri slept with his fathers, and was buried in
Samaria: and Ahab his son reigned in his
stead. . . .

And Ahab the son of Omri did evil in the sight
of the Lord above all that were before him.

Each king, you see, excelled his predecessor
in wickedness and incompetence. We have no
time for them in this rapid survey except for a
single glance at two of the most dramatic
figures—Jezebel, the strong-minded old queen,
and Jehu, who slew her. Jezebel was a princess
of the proud kingdom of Tyre, and when Ahab,
king of Israel, married her, he thought he had
achieved a great diplomatic victory. As Queen
Mother, Jezebel's powerful influence lasted after
the death of her husband and throughout the
reign of her son Joram, king of Israel, and
Azariah, her son-in-law, who was king in Jerusalem. Attaliah was another Jezebel and dom-
inated Jerusalem as the mother did Samaria.
Jehu was a kind of Cromwell, stern, bloody, un-
merciful. He killed both Kings Joram and
Azariah, and raced back to the capital to make
away with Jezebel and all the members of the

royal family. When Jehu started for a place he arrived in a hurry.

> The driving is like the driving of Jehu the son of Nimshi; for he driveth furiously.

Jezebel could have fled, but her queenly pride scorned such cowardice. Instead, she

> painted her face, and tired her head, and looked out at a window.

When Jehu drove through the streets she taunted him as a dog who had slain his master. And Jehu

> lifted up his face to the window, and said, Who is on my side? who? And there looked out to him two or three eunuchs.
> And he said, Throw her down. So they threw her down: and some of her blood was sprinkled on the wall, and on the horses; and he trode her under foot.

With such edifying spectacles the record is thickly dotted. The Hebrew writers were nothing if not honest; they give us the story in all its ignominy and shame. The kings of Jerusalem make a little better showing than the kings of Israel, but we have to remember that the record is written from the Jerusalem point of view. Neither set deserves a place in our memories. Their doings are significant only as a dark background for the shining words and works of the prophets, one of the most remarkable succession of men in human history. It was a case of

> Right forever on the scaffold, wrong forever on the throne
> Yet that scaffold holds the future, and behind the great unknown
> Standeth God within the shadow, keeping watch above his own.

In every wicked reign there was a righteous man of God who could be neither bribed nor intimidated. He stood forth crying "Thus saith the Lord," and though the king writhed and fumed and sought to destroy, the prophet was the victor.

The first of this exalted company was Nathan, who was court preacher in the reign of David. When that mighty monarch had stolen the wife of the brave soldier Uriah and compounded the crime by sending Uriah into the front line of the battle, Nathan appeared at the court and announced that he had come to tell the king a story. There were two men in a certain city, he said, the one rich, having many flocks and herds, and the other so poor that he possessed only one little ewe lamb. And the rich man, desiring a banquet, had spared all of his own big flocks and appropriated the poor man's one lamb.

> And David's anger was greatly kindled against the man; and he said to Nathan, As the Lord liveth, the man that hath done this thing shall surely die. . . .
> And Nathan said to David, *Thou art the man.*

Picture to yourself the spectacle. The king on his golden throne surrounded by his lords and soldiers; the penniless preacher, clothed in rough skins, with no power but Truth, no protection but the flaming sword of moral courage. *"Thou art the man."* The effect was immediate.

> And David said unto Nathan, I have sinned against the Lord.
> . . . and David fasted, and went in, and lay all night upon the earth.

After Nathan came Elijah the Tishbite, a hairy man, living alone in the woods, drinking the water of mountain streams, and fed by ravens. He it was who stood out against the four hundred prophets of the religion of Baal which the wicked Queen Jezebel had imported, and challenged them to a life and death contest. They were to build their altar and lay their sacrifice thereon; he would lay a similar sacrifice on the altar of the Lord. Whichever god sent down fire from

Heaven was the one who deserved to be worshiped. From morning until noon the false prophets leaped upon their altar, calling out to Baal, while Elijah taunted them.

> And it came to pass at noon, that Elijah mocked them, and said, Cry aloud: for he is a god; either he is talking, or he is pursuing, or he is in a journey, or peradventure he sleepeth and must be awaked.

At evening when the four hundred had proved their inability to deliver the goods, Elijah laid up his own altar, placed the sacrifice on it, stacked up the wood, and poured water over it to make the test harder. Then he prayed.

> Then the fire of the Lord fell, and consumed the burnt sacrifice, and the wood, and the stones, and the dust, and licked up the water that was in the trench.
> And when all the people saw it, they fell on their faces: and they said, The Lord, he is the God; the Lord, he is the God.
> And Elijah said unto them, Take the prophets of Baal; let not one of them escape. And they took them: and Elijah brought them down to the brook Kishon, and slew them there.

He knew well that the same fate would have befallen him had he lost, and indeed it threatened him anyway. Queen Jezebel was nothing if not courageous, as we have already seen. When she heard what he had done to her prophets she

> sent a messenger to Elijah saying, So let the gods do to me, and more also, if I make not thy life as the life of one of them by to morrow about this time.

Elijah was forced to flee, and suffered a breakdown from which he never fully recovered. But he had strength enough left to plant himself squarely across the path of King Ahab. That royal gentleman desired to extend his estate and tried to buy the vineyard of a self-respecting citizen named Naboth, who refused to sell. Ahab caused Naboth to be accused of treason, and he was put to death, and his estate, according to the law, was confiscated. King Ahab hurried over to look at his new acreage, and there was Elijah waiting for him.

> And Ahab said to Elijah, Hast thou found me, O, mine enemy? And he answered, I have found thee; because thou hast sold thyself to work evil in the sight of the Lord.
> Behold I will bring evil upon thee, and will take away thy posterity. . . .
> And it came to pass, when Ahab heard these words that he rent his clothes, and put sackcloth upon his flesh, and fasted, and lay in sackcloth, and went softly.

All the starch went out of the kings when the prophets spoke up. Elijah was one of the most heroic of them all, and Mount Carmel, where he faced the idol worshipers, is a monument on the path of human progress. It marks the spot where one man stood against tremendous odds and by his own single-handed courage turned back a nation to spiritual worship. Of him we might say what Whittier wrote of another champion of righteousness:

> The world redeemed from superstition's sway
> Is breathing freer for thy sake to-day.

We are told that Elijah never died but was snatched up to Heaven in a chariot of fire. Elisha, who had been his assistant, put on his mantle and continued his work, a power in the land for many years. So great was his vitality that even death could not destroy it.

> And it came to pass, as they were burying a man that, behold, they spied a band of men; and they cast the man into the sepulchre of Elisha; and when the man was let down, and touched the bones of Elisha, he revived, and stood up on his feet.

The earlier prophets did not write their sermons, but about 800 B. C. some of them began

doing so. The first to write was Amos. He
was not trained in a theological school and did
not belong to the priestly party or wear the
union label, so that when he began to preach an
officious priest tried to stop him. Amos would
not be stopped; he had plenty of courage. A
little later we shall refer to him again, and to
Hosea, who belongs to the same period. The
prophets seem to have come in pairs—

Amos and Hosea,
Isaiah and Micah,
Ezekiel and Jeremiah.

Micah was a down-state man who had the
same prejudice against Jerusalem that many
people now feel toward New York. It was
hopelessly wicked, he said, and merited destruction for its sins:

> Therefore shall Zion for your sake be plowed
> as a field, and Jerusalem shall become heaps, and
> the mountain of the house as the high places of the
> forest.

Isaiah, on the contrary, was a city man, loving
town life, at home in the bustle of the market-
place and the activities of the court. Jerusalem
was a grand town to live in, he said, in spite of
its sins, and God would take care of it.

> Therefore saith the Lord . . . I will defend

this city to save it for mine own sake, and for my servant David's sake.

These two quotations encourage us with the knowledge—much needed in these controversial days—that two men can be equally good and acceptable to God and yet hold absolutely contradictory views. Micah and Isaiah agreed in their stern insistence upon righteousness as the only path to salvation, but they disagreed violently in respect to Jerusalem. Both were right and both wrong. God *did* defend the city for a long time after the northern kingdom surrendered to its enemies in 722 B. C. But ultimately, in 586 B. C., the destruction which Micah had prophesied came true. The beautiful temple of Solomon was laid in ruins, and the proudest families of Jerusalem were carried away captive to Babylon.

In speaking of Micah and Isaiah as a pair, we mean that they lived at the same time, not that they were on the same level, intellectually or in the importance of their message. Isaiah was one of the outstanding religious leaders of all history. He was of high birth, and may even have been related to the royal family, for he had free access to the palace, and he appears to have been a preceptor for one king, Hezekiah. His ministry began in "the year that King Uzziah died," the king who had been his hero and whose reign, brilliantly begun, ended lamentably.

Isaiah had to rebuke sin in high places, to offend princes and priests and politicians, for he belonged to the stormy period when the Assyrians were invading adjacent realms, and his own little kingdom was trying vainly to make its future secure by an alliance with Egypt. This he denounced and thereby gained the ill-will of many powerful interests. But when the time came that Jerusalem needed Egypt's help, Egypt had her own hands more than full. On a desperately tragic day the Assyrian army camped before Jerusalem, and the king and his counselors were in terror. The king covered himself with sackcloth and sent for Isaiah, the one unterrified man in town.

Isaiah's day had come. He wasted no time rubbing in his reproaches, but spoke with a voice which put new courage into the king and all his forces.

> Therefore thus saith the Lord concerning the king of Assyria, He shall not come into this city, nor shoot an arrow there, nor come before it with shields, nor cast a bank against it.
>
> By the way that he came, by the same shall he return, and shall not come into this city, saith the Lord. . . .

77

> Then the angel of the Lord went forth, and
> smote in the camp of the Assyrians a hundred and
> fourscore and five thousand: and when they arose
> early in the morning, behold, they were all dead
> corpses.

We are not dependent upon the Bible alone
for the story of this invasion. Scientists in their
probings into ancient records have found the account written by Sennacherib, the Assyrian king,
himself, and his own confession that the expedition failed to capture Jerusalem.

While Isaiah denounced both Assyria and
Egypt, and urged Jerusalem to avoid entangling
alliances with either of them, he had a conception
of international relations which is amazingly
modern in the best sense of the word.

> In that day shall there be a highway out of
> Egypt to Assyria, and the Assyrian shall come
> into Egypt, and the Egyptian into Assyria, and
> the Egyptians shall serve with the Assyrians.
> In that day shall Israel be the third with Egypt
> and with Assyria, even a blessing in the midst of
> the land:
> Whom the Lord of hosts shall bless, saying,
> Blessed be Egypt my people, and Assyria the
> work of my hands, and Israel mine inheritance.

This is precisely as if, while we were still at
war with Germany, having Great Britain as our
nearest ally, we had said: "Some day the war

will be over and the Divine plan will include and need us all. The United States is to be one of three powers in the future glory of the world, and the other two are to be Great Britain and Germany, for the Lord has blessed them all, saying, 'Blessed be England my people, and Germany the work of my hands, and America mine inheritance.' "

Isaiah had to be a pessimist as to the immediate future, but his superb optimism is shown all through his work, and comes to its worthiest expression in the poem with which his own book of sermons ends:

> Strengthen ye the weak hands, and confirm the feeble knees.
> Say to them that are of a fearful heart, Be strong, fear not: behold, your God will come . .
> Then the eyes of the blind shall be opened, and the ears of the deaf shall be unstopped:
> Then shall the lame man leap as an hart, and the tongue of the dumb sing: for in the wilderness shall waters break out, and streams in the desert.
> And the parched ground shall become a pool, and the thirsty land springs of water . . .

When we say that Isaiah's own book ends with this magnificent poem, somebody raises an objection. "The book of Isaiah has sixty-six chapters,"

he says, "and how can it end with chapter 35?"
The answer is that beginning with chapter 40,
this book has another author. We do not know
his name, nor why he took such great pains to
conceal it. Following the exile one hundred years
or more after the work and writing of Isaiah
himself, there were some useful but rather
commonplace prophets, Haggai and Zechariah,
whose messages helped on the work of rebuilding the temple, but who can not be called
great men. But one truly great voice did speak
out, the voice of this splendid Unknown, the
author of the last chapters of the book which is
all labeled with Isaiah's name. It was he who
proclaimed that the time had come to build a road
back to Jerusalem and to restore the devastated
city.

He described himself as "the voice of a herald"
crying, "Make straight in the desert a highway
for our God." He called men to grade the roads,
cutting down the hills and filling the valleys
and preparing to go back to Zion. He does
not name Isaiah nor refer to any king or event
contemporary with him. On the contrary, these
chapters were clearly written a hundred and fifty
years later, in the time of Cyrus, the new king of
Persia, and the Unknown sees in his rise to
power a divinely given opportunity.

> Thus saith the Lord to his anointed, to Cyrus, whose right hand I have holden, to subdue nations before him; . . .
>
> I will go before thee, and make the crooked places straight: I will break in pieces the gates of brass, and cut in sunder the bars of iron:
>
> And I will give thee the treasures of darkness, and hidden riches of secret places, that thou mayest know that I, the Lord, which call thee by thy name, am the God of Israel.
>
> For Jacob my servant's sake, and Israel mine elect, I have even called thee by thy name: I have surnamed thee, though thou hast not known me.

Even though Cyrus was a heathen, he was God's Messiah for that event. Talk if you like about being broad-minded! Then think of the prejudices that prophet had to overcome to make such a declaration. And think what came of it: a new nation, a new and purer worship, a new epoch in the spiritual history of mankind.

Here is his vision for the rebuilding of Jerusalem:

> Arise, shine; for thy light is come, and the glory of the Lord is risen upon thee.
>
> For, behold, the darkness shall cover the earth, and gross darkness the people: but the Lord shall arise upon thee, and his glory shall be seen upon thee.
>
> And the Gentiles shall come to thy light, and kings to the brightness of thy rising.

And this is his dream of a regenerate society and a peaceful world; a new heaven and earth, that is, a new theology and a new political economy:

For, behold, I create new heavens and a new earth: and the former shall not be remembered, nor come into mind.

But be ye glad and rejoice for ever in that which I create: for, behold, I create Jerusalem a rejoicing, and her people a joy.

And I will rejoice in Jerusalem, and joy in my people: and the voice of weeping shall be no more heard in her, nor the voice of crying.

There shall be no more thence an infant of days, nor an old man that hath not filled his days: for the child shall die an hundred years old; but the sinner being an hundred years old shall be accursed.

And they shall build houses, and inhabit them; and they shall plant vineyards, and eat the fruit of them.

They shall not build, and another inhabit; they shall not plant, and another eat: for as the days of a tree are the days of my people, and mine elect shall long enjoy the work of their hands.

They shall not labour in vain, nor bring forth for trouble; for they are the seed of the blessed of the Lord, and their offspring with them.

And it shall come to pass, that before they call, I will answer: and while they are yet speaking, I will hear.

The wolf and the lamb shall feed together, and

the lion shall eat straw like the bullock: and dust shall be the serpent's meat. They shall not hurt nor destroy in all my holy mountain, saith the Lord.

These are words of splendor, and it is a pity that the author of them should have been so determined to conceal his identity and so successful in doing it.

Between the days of Isaiah himself and the times of the Unknown whose chapters conclude the book came the dark period of the exile, when Jerusalem was destroyed and its best families carried away captive to Babylon. To this dark period Ezekiel and Jeremiah belong. Ezekiel living in Babylon, sought by his exhortations to keep up the spirit of his fellow-countrymen and fix their hopes upon a restoration of the Holy City and the reestablishment of their national life. Jeremiah, in Jerusalem, held high the ideal of personal and civic righteousness and spoke plain truths to the vassal king, who was allowed by the conquerors to maintain a pitiful remnant of authority and kingly show.

Jeremiah is one of the noblest characters of history and perhaps the bravest figure in the whole Old Testament. It is too bad that his book is so badly mixed up that the average reader can hardly follow it. He preached in the temple and in the palace and on the street corners, and even on the city dump; and neither promises nor threats could swerve him. Jehoiakim, the weak and futile king, let the temple go to ruin but fixed up his own palace with a rich lining of cedar and invited Jeremiah to inspect it.

"Very nice indeed," sneered Jeremiah. "As a king you're a fine judge of cedar. Your father did justice to the poor and needy, and it was well with him."

> But thine eyes and thine heart are not but for thy covetousness, and for to shed innocent blood, and for oppression and for violence to do it.
> Therefore thus saith the Lord concerning Jehoiakim . . . He shall be buried with the burial of an ass, drawn and cast forth beyond the gates of Jerusalem.

For such plain speaking and for his warnings that the Assyrians were sure to visit punishment upon the city, Jeremiah was cast into prison. Then occurred one of the most interesting business transactions of the Old Testament. The Assyrians, as Jeremiah had prophesied, *did* come, and they made their camp in Anathoth, where he had his own little farm. Jeremiah had long wanted to buy an adjoining piece of land owned by a relative, Hanameel. That wily old man, seeing an army of Assyrians camped on the land, said to himself: "Jeremiah is down there in prison and probably hasn't heard that the Assyrians have arrived. This is a good time for me to unload on him." So he hurried to the prison, offered the land, and Jeremiah bought it. But Jeremiah was not fooled. He knew he was buying ten thousand Assyrians and he took care to have the purchase properly recorded in the presence of witnesses, and the documents safely put away.

> Thus saith the Lord of hosts [he exclaimed], the God of Israel; Take these evidences, this evidence of the purchase, both which is sealed, and this evidence which is open: and put them in an earthen vessel, that they may continue many days.
> For thus saith the Lord of hosts, the God of Israel; *Houses and fields and vineyards shall be possessed again in this land.*

The punishment which he had foretold as a result of national sin had come, but he knew that a period of national calamity brings repentance followed by better days, and that the time to trust in the Lord and buy good real estate is when everybody else has lost faith and is eager to sell. We shall refer again to Jeremiah when we come to discuss the Bible's ten greatest men.

Every one who has read the Old Testament

at all knows about Daniel, who spent a night with the lions rather than give up his religion; and about Shadrach, Meshach and Abednego, his three sturdy associates. They were cast into a fiery furnace but walked comfortably upon the hot coals and came forth without even smelling of smoke. Similarly, we are well acquainted with Esther, the beautiful Jewess, who became queen and had the satisfaction of seeing Haman, the wicked prime minister, hung upon the high gallows which he had built for Mordecai the Jew. These are two heroic figures, Daniel and Esther, and it is sad indeed to be told that the scientists, in digging around among the ruins of those far-away times, have been unable to find any trace of a prime minister named Daniel or a queen called Esther. We are forced reluctantly to conclude that the two books bearing these honored names are splendid pieces of Jewish propaganda, written by patriotic gentlemen who sought to uphold the spirits of their fellow-exiles and, in the case of Daniel, nerve them for one of the most heroic struggles in history—one that in spite of overwhelming odds succeeded.

As with Daniel, so with Esther. The author of the book that bears her name made her victory complete, as we shall have occasion to note more fully when we come back to her again. You will remember that her uncle Mordecai, a Jew, was prime minister.

> And Mordecai went out from the presence of the king in royal apparel of blue and white, and with a great crown of gold, and with a garment of fine linen and purple and . . .
> The Jews had light, and gladness, and joy, and honour. . . .
> And many of the people of the land became Jews; for the fear of the Jews came upon them.

But these verses which make so brave a showing for the Jews, are not an historic document; only a pious hope. The Jews, in reading them, buckled their belts a little tighter and took courage. We can read the book of Esther and the book of Daniel with pleasure and appreciation, not as history but just as we read other dramatic stories which deserve to be called truly great.

In taking leave of the Old Testament we must stop to pay reverent tribute to two great truths which give eternal significance to these ancient books.

1. We have in the record of the division and downfall of the Jewish nation the first instance in human history where the god did not go with the land. In earlier days each tribe and nation

had its own particular deity or set of deities, and when a man transferred from one country to another he, of course, changed gods. Naomi, urging her two beautiful daughters-in-law to go back to their own country after their husbands had died of starvation, said to Ruth:

> Behold, thy sister-in-law is gone back unto her people, *and unto her gods*: return thou after thy sister-in-law.

It was assumed that when a woman married she took the gods of her husband; if he died and she must go back to her own people, she abandoned her husband's gods and took theirs again. But when the ten tribes of Israel split away from the tribes of Judah and Benjamin, Jehovah did not go to either one or the other, *but remained with both*. His worship was often neglected, but in their hearts the people knew that He was still their God and always at the time of tribulation they threw down their idols and returned to Him.

The idea of One God—unseen and not to be worshiped in visible form—had been born in the world, and had taken firm hold upon human minds. This is the outstanding achievement of the Hebrews, the thing which gives the Old Testament eternal truth and inspiration.

2. In its total effect the Old Testament is a
record of God's progressive revelation of Himself to men. This is the second element in its
greatness. Steadily from Genesis to Micah the
conception of His nature and quality grows
clearer, bigger, finer.

A God who had to be persuaded by argument
and sacrifices, who drove hard bargains with
any who sought to disobey or cheat Him—this
was the God of Abraham, of Isaac and of Jacob.
But gradually other thinking began to stir in the
minds of men, and find expression in the courageous utterances of the prophets. We have
referred already to Amos, who was not a priest
and had nothing but scorn for the formulæ and
ritual of the established religion. He saw the
temple courtyards red with blood and men seek-
ing through sacrifices to buy the right to be
iniquitous, and he cried out: "God cares nothing
for sacrifice; He is a God of Justice."

I hate, I despise your feast days, and I will not
smell in your solemn assemblies.

Though ye offer me burnt offerings and your
meat offerings, I will not accept them: neither will
I regard the peace offerings of your fat beasts.

Take thou away from me the noise of thy songs;
for I will not hear the melody of thy viols.

But let judgment run down as waters, and
righteousness as a mighty stream.

As a conception of the Almighty this represented a vast step upward. In those same days
another preacher, Hosea, was adding another
item to the expanding fund of truth. Hosea
was a married man, and his wife was a flirt. The
town was full of gossip about her, so much so
that Hosea was compelled finally to put her
away. His friends said "good riddance," and
even the most critical agreed that he had been
amply justified in his action. But Hosea, but-
tressed about by public opinion, was none the
less torn by lonesomeness, sorrow and regret.
This woman who had wronged him—he still
loved her, wanted her, could not live without
her. Pocketing his pride he went to her with
forgiveness and took her back to his home.

And out of that domestic tragedy there came
to Hosea a great new truth. "If I, being only
a man, can love so much and forgive so much,
surely God must be capable of even more," he
said. Amos had told the world that God is just;
Hosea added, *"and kind."*

In Isaiah and Jeremiah we find the new
thought of God's kindness gaining added force,
but the book of Jonah gives the most interesting
and probably the least appreciated glimpse of
the development of the idea. Because of Jonah's
mishap, which resulted in a three days' sojourn

in the belly of a big fish, that book of four little chapters has been too often passed over lightly or treated with contempt. It deserves recognition and reverence, for it contains the most compassionate note in the Old Testament.

Jonah was a preacher, you remember, and was ordered by God to go to Nineveh and denounce the city for its sins. Instead of carrying out his orders Jonah ran away, was caught in a storm at sea, thrown overboard by the panic-stricken sailors, and held in the belly of a great fish until he was thoroughly repentant and ready to obey. After this severe lesson he went to Nineveh and announced to all and sundry that the city would be destroyed for its sins within forty days. So convincing were his words and manner that the rulers of the city ordered a general period of fasting and repentance.

> Who can tell [they cried] if God will turn and repent, and turn away from his fierce anger, and we perish not? And God saw their works, that they turned from their evil way; and God repented of the evil, that he had said he would do unto them; and he did it not.

This was good luck for the people of Nineveh but it was hard on Jonah and "he was very angry." He reproached God, saying, "I knew you wouldn't go through with your threat and that's why I tried to run away from this assignment"

> for I knew that thou art a gracious God, and merciful, slow to anger, and of great kindness, and repentest thee of the evil.

He went outside the city and sat down in a chair to watch and sulk and to see what would happen. The sun was hot and God caused a great gourd to grow up over Jonah and shelter him. But the next morning when Jonah thought he should be sitting pretty, God sent a worm to cut the stem of the gourd and it withered away. Then come the final three verses which picture Jehovah in a nobler, more compassionate character than any of the Old Testament writers had ever pictured him before:

> And God said to Jonah, Doest thou well to be angry for the gourd? And he said, I do well to be angry, even unto death.
> Then said the Lord, Thou hast had pity on the gourd, for which thou hast not laboured, neither madest it grow; which came up in a night, and perished in a night:
> And should not I spare Nineveh, that great city, wherein are more than sixscore thousand persons that cannot discern between their right hand and their left hand; and also much cattle?

What a noble utterance. What a long up-

ward climb has been made since the days when
the Israelites plundered cities and wiped out
men, women and children under the conviction
that they were working the will of God. The
record of this upward progress *is* the Old Testament. It begins with savage people, merciless
prophets, and a terrible God.

> Thus saith the Lord of hosts, I remember that
> which Amalek did to Israel, how he laid wait for
> him in the way, when he came up from Egypt.
> Now go and smite Amalek, and utterly destroy
> all that they have, and spare them not; but slay
> both man and woman, infant and suckling, ox and
> sheep, camel and ass.

And it ends with a people who have learned
humility through suffering and righteousness
through adversity, and with prophets who utter
the will of God in more and more exalted language, ending with Micah who reached the
grandest elevation of all.

> He hath shewed thee, O man, what is good; and
> what doth the Lord require of thee, but to do
> justly, and to love mercy, and to walk humbly
> with thy God.

III
THE GREAT LIFE

QUESTIONS

1. What is the shortest verse in the Bible?
   John 11:35.

2. Who were the three Marys in the life of Jesus?
   Luke 1:27; John 12:3; John 20:18.

3. Where is the account of the Sermon on the Mount?
   Matthew 5, 6, 7.

4. What is the origin of the phrase, "a doubting Thomas"?
   John 20:24-27.

5. How do we know that the same man who wrote the Gospel according to St. Luke also wrote the Acts of the Apostles?
   Luke 1:1-4; Acts 1:1-4.

6. What two disciples were called the "sons of thunder"?
   Mark 3:17.

7. Of all the miracles of Jesus which one is recorded by all the Evangelists?
   Matthew 14:13-21; Mark 6:31-44; Luke 9:12-17; John 6:1-14.

8. Where is the parable of the Prodigal Son? What other parables are in the same chapter?
   Luke 15.

9. What became of Judas who betrayed his Lord?
   Matthew 27:5.

10. Where is the Golden Rule?
    Matthew 7:12.

III

THE GREAT LIFE

ONE spring evening just nineteen hundred
years ago a band of hard-faced men stole out of
Jerusalem, crossed a little valley and made
their way into the Garden of Gethsemane.
Armed with clubs and spears, they carried
torches which cast weird shadows through the
trees, and, though they doubtless tried to move
quietly, the noise of their progress must have
jangled cruelly in the peace of that lovely night.
At the gate that opened into a garden on the
slope of the hill stood Jesus of Nazareth await-
ing them. A pathetic little company of disciples
trembled about Him, but, as the heavy steps
drew closer and the spear points gleamed in the
flickering light, the disciples melted away until
He was left alone.

Not quite alone.

And there followed him a certain young man,
having a linen cloth cast about his naked body;
and the young men [soldiers or members of the
mob] laid hold on him;

And he left the linen cloth, and fled from them
naked.

These words are our introduction to an important historical character. The young man who left his linen cloth and fled naked was Mark, author of the so-called "second Gospel," which, in point of composition, is actually the first. Before any other mind had thought of it, he conceived the grand idea of making a written record of the works and words of Jesus. Subsequent New Testament writers were debtors to young Mark, and so are we all.

He was not one of the original twelve disciples; indeed, he may never have seen Jesus except on that fateful night. His mother was a believer, and the Last Supper was held at her house. You can picture the active-minded boy, lying curious in his bed in the family room downstairs, overhearing the wonderful farewell words of Jesus, the final hymn, and the rustle of preparation for departure. On the impulse of the moment he jumped out of bed and followed to the Garden. Whether he was a witness to any of the events of the next few days we have no means of knowing. We do know, however, that he was associated for a time with Paul and later with Peter. Hearing them talk about Jesus, gathering an incident here and a saying there, he began gradually to compose his book. It is a brief straightforward story, with brisk action

and very little discourse, just those high spots
of activity and achievement that would appeal
most naturally to a young man.

For a time his book was the only life of Jesus.
Then a Jew named Matthew, apparently the
same man who had been a tax collector and was
called to discipleship, looked it over and said to
himself: "This book would be much more useful if it had a lot of Old Testament references.
And, besides, it ought to have more of what
Jesus said." So he made these additions,
sprinkling his narrative with the phrase, "that
it might be fulfilled as was written by the
prophets." His book contains the word "fulfilled" more times than any of the others; it is
obvious that he was bent on giving the life of
Jesus all the Old Testament authority possible
and that his object was to write what might be
termed "The Gospel (or Good News) as
Adapted to Jewish Readers."

Paul, the most adventurous of the early
Christian missionaries, was often sick, and had
as a physician a Greek gentleman named Luke.
Luke had a friend named Theophilus who, as
he thought, would be interested in the story of
Jesus, but not in the form set forth by Mark or
Matthew. Accordingly, Luke wrote:

Forasmuch as many have taken in hand to set forth in order a declaration of those things which are most surely believed among us,

Even as they delivered them unto us, which from the beginning were eyewitnesses, and ministers of the word;

It seemed good to me also, having had perfect understanding of all things from the very first, to write unto thee in order, most excellent Theophilus.

You will note that he does not criticize the accounts already written but observes merely that he does not find them adapted to Theophilus. He did not claim to have been, and in fact was not, an original disciple, but he said that he had enjoyed exceptional opportunities for hearing the story from reliable men who had first-hand knowledge. These are perfectly straightforward reasons for writing a book and they furnish a pleasing introduction both to the Good News as Luke wrote it and to that later book, partly compiled from his own experiences as a companion of Paul, the Acts of the Apostles.

Luke did not care a fig about quotations from the Old Testament which might be very convincing to a Jew, for Theophilus was not a Jew. But he did tell of the Good Samaritan, and of the Prodigal Son, and some other exalted stories of the appreciation of Jesus for folks beyond the narrow walls of Judaism. Matthew never could have written this book any more than Luke could have written Matthew's.

One other fact is significant about the third Gospel. In some way the writer got hold of a fresh source of information about the women of that early Jerusalem community. Who told him and what was told we can only guess, but the fact is clear that Luke knew more and tells more about the women who were friends of Jesus than any of the other writers. That element gives an added quality of fineness to his book, which is probably the most beautiful book in the world.

Years later, in Ephesus, where Greek philosophy had tinged the thought and vocabulary of all educated people, a man named John wrote another story of Jesus. It is hardly the life-story; rather is it an interpretation, and a very fine one. We should have lost some of the most beautiful sayings of Jesus if it were not for this fourth Gospel, and one has only to read it through to understand why in every age it has been so greatly loved.

These four books have much duplication, and this was an inconvenience when copying had to be done by hand, so that very early in the history of the church there began to be made compilations like Tatian's *Diatessaron,* which attempted to cut up the four books and knit them together into a connected story. We may be glad that none of these attempts proved successful and that, with all their duplication and occasional contradictions, we have these different records in their original form, with the earmarks of their separate authorship perfectly clear. The four are a hundred times more convincing than one account could possibly be, and the very fact that they do not always agree is the best possible proof that they tell a real and not a manufactured story.

A few weeks ago two young men desiring to enter the Christian ministry were asked, "Do you believe in the Virgin Birth of Jesus?" Upon replying that they did not know how to answer the question, nor regard the answer as vital to their work as ministers, they were rejected.

It is no part of the purpose of our little book to deal with controversial subjects, but in approaching the life of Jesus we may perhaps be permitted to point out that the question of whether He was or was not born of a virgin did not seem very important to two of the writers of the Gospels. Mark makes no mention of it. John ignores it. Paul does not once refer to it, and if Jesus Himself was much concerned there is no evidence of that fact. When He was assembling His disciples, He called a certain Philip of Bethsaida:

> Philip findeth Nathanael, and saith unto him, We have found him, of whom Moses in the law, and the prophets, did write, Jesus of Nazareth, *the son of Joseph.*

If this assertion on the part of Philip was a mistake Jesus did not rebuke it nor refuse Philip and Nathanael as disciples because of it. Indeed, one astonishing fact about His life and the doctrines which have been built up about it is this—that most of the points on which the bitter controversies have been waged were apparently regarded by Jesus Himself as of lesser significance, and some of them of no significance whatever.

How many cruel debates have arisen over the question of His miracles. Yet nothing is clearer than that He did not attach the same importance to these mighty works as His followers did. He was often reluctant to perform them, and was so fearful that He might be advertised abroad as a wonder-worker and thus have the real significance of His teaching blurred that He frequently urged those whom he had healed to "go and tell no man."

The question of baptism has split Christian communions. Jesus, when His success began to bring great crowds to Him so that His disciples were baptizing more than John the Baptist, ceased Himself to baptize anybody.

> When therefore the Lord knew how the Pharisees had heard that Jesus made and baptized more disciples than John,
> (Though Jesus himself baptized not, but his disciples,)
> He left Judæa, and departed again into Galilee.

The question of forms and ceremonies and revisions of prayer-books occupies the time and discussion of many church assemblies. But there is no record that Jesus ever prayed in public. The one prayer which He gave to His disciples is the simplest imaginable and consists of sixty-six words. As for the place and manner and form of worship, He dismissed the whole subject with one great and unforgettable sentence. It was a part of one of the most remarkable discourses of His ministry, delivered to an audience of one, the woman of Samaria. Said she:

> Our fathers worshipped in this mountain; and ye [being a Jew] say, that in Jerusalem is the place where men ought to worship.

104

To which Jesus answered:

> Woman, believe me, the hour cometh, when ye shall neither in this mountain, nor yet at Jerusalem, worship the Father. . . .
> God is a Spirit: and they that worship him must worship him *in spirit and in truth.*

He was much more tolerant toward heretical opinions than were any of His followers, either those of His immediate circle or those who have taken His name in later days. His attitude was set forth clearly on the day when one of His disciples came boasting that he had found a man doing good in His name and, since this man was an outsider and not of their own number, the disciple had forbidden him. He doubtless expected praise, but he met a rebuke.

> Jesus said, . . . Forbid him not; for he that is not against us is for us.

His was the broadest sort of invitation to fellowship, having no petty barriers of creed or formulæ or ceremony. "He went about doing good." "Never man so spake." These—His good works and His good words—are the things for which He wished to be remembered; they constitute the story of His life.

He was born in troubled times. In previous chapters we have traced the rise of the Jews from their beginning as nomadic shepherds to their glory as a nation under David and Solomon (about 1000 B. C.). We have seen the kingdom split into two parts, and the long sad years of bickerings, intrigues, foreign entanglements and decline, eventuating in the capture of Jerusalem and the exile of its leading families into Babylon. In this running survey we have no time to trace the various reestablishments of the sacred city—though this means the elimination of some fine figures, such as Nehemiah—nor its various phases of destruction. The successive conquerors of the ancient world reached their climax in Alexander, who overran more territory than any of them and, weeping because there were no more worlds to conquer, died of dissipation in his early thirties in 323 B. C.

Immediately his vast kingdom was broken up. That part of it which included Palestine came under the control first of Egypt in the days of the Ptolemies, who built the great library at Alexandria, translated the Old Testament into Greek in the version known as the Septuagint (work of seventy scholars), and opened a home in Egypt for many thousands of Jews. Egyptian domination gave place to that of the sporadic Grecianized Syrian kingdom, in which King Antiochus is the most interesting figure to us, since his tyranny inspired the revolt of the Maccabees.

The Maccabæan family, a heroic Jewish priest and his seven brave sons, began a war with no higher hope than that of dying for the faith, and they achieved the impossible result of winning the freedom of their country. Again a race of Jewish kings ruled in Jerusalem, this in the middle of the second century before Christ (about 150 B. C., as a rough easy date). A sturdy little kingdom it was but unable to stand very long against invaders from without and political and religious decay within. Inevitably it came under the conquering power of Rome, but the vigor of the Maccabees promised to perpetuate itself in a new line of kings. Herod, a military leader from across Jordan, allied himself with Rome and was made a kind of feudal king. He married a Maccabæan princess, Mariamne, whose beauty and tragic fate gripped the imaginations of the people and made the name Mary so common in New Testament times and later. Herod murdered her, and she was only one among his many victims.

Rome passed from a nominal republic into an empire. Cæsar Augustus was Emperor and Herod (beneficiary of the brave Maccabees) reigned in Palestine when Jesus was born.

The policy of Rome was tolerant; local customs and even local prejudices were not greatly interfered with, and the Jews were permitted to carry on their worship and, to a large extent, the internal affairs of their government as they chose under their own rulers. But Rome was the power that ruled, and naturally the Jews were not happy. They had become a nation whose ideals were bound up in a book. If they no longer had their independence they still did have the Law, the Prophets and the Writings. They studied these and thought they found promises that Jerusalem was again to have political power. They looked back to the days of David and Solomon, idealizing the reigns of these great kings. They were sure that some day another king of David's lineage would sit on the throne in their sacred city and they even found in Micah a verse which some imagined to mean that their king would be born in Bethlehem:

> But thou, Beth-lehem Ephratah, though thou be little among the thousands of Judah, yet out of thee shall he come forth unto me that is to be ruler in Israel; whose goings forth have been from of old, from everlasting.

It is necessary to have this little historic background in order to understand why there were

two rulers simultaneously in the days of Jesus:
Herod the King, whom Jesus characterized as
"that fox," and Pilate, the Roman governor;
and why the Jewish crowds, fired by patriotic
enthusiasm, sought to take Jesus, "Son of
David," by force and make Him their king; and
why, when He refused, they melted away from
Him and allowed the shouts of "Hosanna" of
Palm Sunday to be drowned out on Friday by
the shout of "Crucify."

This little book is being written in the year
1926. As nearly as scholars can figure it out,
Jesus was born about 4 B. C. The Christian
chronology was not fixed until the sixth century,
and our subsequent study of the Roman records
which mention the great taxation in the reign
of Cæsar Augustus indicates that a mistake of
about four years was made. Assuming the date
4 B. C., therefore, we approach now (1926) the
nineteen hundredth anniversary of Jesus' thir-
tieth birthday, the time when a man became fully
of age in that country where parental authority
lasted longer than it does here. It is not impossible that the very hour at which this page
was written may mark the anniversary of the
great decision which changed Him from a
humble carpenter into the greatest Teacher of
the world.

The preceding years of His life are cloaked in mystery. We catch one glimpse of Him going up to the Temple with His parents, where He was lost from them for a day and subsequently discovered in the midst of a group of wise old men, asking questions and amazing them by the keen penetration of His comment. Except for this single episode the Gospels throw very little light upon His boyhood. We know the names of His brothers, James and Judas and Joses and Simon, and there were at least two sisters. For some years He apparently was the man of the house, and His earnings in the carpenter shop were the main support of the family. Perhaps this was a disappointment to Him, for He must have been a studious boy who would have preferred to read and study. But He was strong and vigorous, and the family needed His help and His younger brothers His protection. At thirty, however, He had discharged His obligations; He was free legally and morally to find His own occupation and to do as He liked.

But what should He do? He had no professional education. He had attended the village school in the synagogue, as every Jewish boy of His time was supposed to do, and He could read, as we know, for He did read later in public; and His conversation and discourses showed a considerable degree of familiarity with the literature of His people, the Law and the Prophets and the Psalms. It requires no great imagination to sense the brooding that must have gone on within Him as He lifted up His eyes from the bench to see a caravan passing through the valley below on its way to the greater world, or sat at night under stars wondering at the eternal mysteries behind them.

One day in the slack season, about the first of the year as we count it, He took a vacation, turned the shop over to His brothers and went away to attend a kind of camp-meeting conducted by His brilliant, fiery young cousin, John. The two cousins had known each other more or less, for John's father was a priest, and there is little doubt that as Jesus went up to Jerusalem for the annual feasts He met John there. John had turned his back on the priesthood and become an independent preacher. It is rather a solemn thought that at nearly every important period of Jewish history the established church failed to meet the requirements of the situation. Neither the prophets nor the psalm writers were official priests, but unsalaried and unofficial. John the Baptist refused the priesthood; Jesus was a layman. This is not necessarily a criticism of organized religion, but it

THE BOOK NOBODY KNOWS

does suggest strongly the need for tolerance in
the church and for a spirit of humanity toward
new truth, whether from inside or outside the
ranks.

John drew great crowds. He must have been
a powerfully dramatic figure, his leathern girdle
about his loins, eating his locusts and wild honey,
and denouncing the eminent Pharisees and
Sadducees as a "generation of vipers."

> Who hath warned you to flee from the wrath
> to come?
> Bring forth therefore fruits meet for repent-
> ance:
> And think not to say within yourselves, We
> have Abraham to our father: for I say unto you,
> that God is able of these stones to raise up chil-
> dren unto Abraham.

Jesus felt the contagion of the movement.
He also went to John and asked to be baptized,
and John looking up and seeing Him on the
bank uttered a noble testimony to the sort of
boy and young man that Jesus must have been:

> I have need to be baptized of thee, and comest
> thou to me?

It is noteworthy that no sense of guilt or
shame appears to have had a part in His religious experience at this point. He did not argue

with John about their relative fitness to baptize each other. He felt that the spirit of devotion which was in Him demanded some outward expression, and John's way, through baptism, was the way that presented itself, and He took advantage of it.

It was a wonderful day for Him. He had made His decision; He had put the old life behind Him. John, His popular and powerful cousin, had recognized His inherent power. From thenceforth He would be a carpenter no longer, but a preacher like John, rebuking men for their sins, calling them to repentance. The day ended, night fell, and with it came the reaction. He went away into the wilderness and remained for more than a month in solitude, tortured by questionings and doubts. He felt power stirring within Him. How should He use it, and for what? The Gospel narrative dramatizes that period of self-searching by the appearance of Satan in person, with a threefold temptation.

And when the tempter came to him, he said, If thou be the Son of God, command that these stones be made bread.

The temptation to use His power for material success—money, comfort, ease.

Then the devil taketh him up into the holy city,
and setteth him on a pinnacle of the temple,
And saith unto him, If thou be the Son of God,
cast thyself down.

The temptation to achieve cheap fame by performing wonders for the admiration of the crowd.

Again, the devil taketh him up into an exceeding high mountain, and sheweth him all the kingdoms of the world, and the glory of them;
And saith unto him, All these things will I give thee, if thou wilt fall down and worship me.

The temptation to become a political leader, to use the popular discontent and His strategic position as a working man's leader as a tool for His own advancement.

To all this He answered, "Get thee behind me, Satan," and He emerged from the wilderness with a clear-cut picture of His mission and His program. He saw very quickly that He could not adopt John's methods. John was an ascetic, a reformer, a denouncer. Jesus was fond of people, loved social life and liked to be in a crowd. John said, "Flee from the wrath to come." Jesus said, "God is your Father, and has made the world as a happy place for His children." The two messages were complementary, but, while the friendship of the cousins was firm and their respect for each other deep and true, they were utterly unlike in personality. Each must speak the truth as he saw it and in his own chosen way.

It was an age when philosophers in cities like Athens and religious teachers in Palestine moved about out-of-doors and gathered as they went from place to place the men who were attracted by their character of learning and wished to become their pupils. It is interesting to remember that the name by which Jesus most liked to be called was "Master," not a master of servants but a master of pupils, a schoolmaster. And the name He gave to His associates, "disciples," means simply "pupils." The story of the way in which He gathered these men is full of interest. He seemed to have no studied method. "As Jesus passed by" He called one and another, saying, "Follow me," and the man who was called left his fishing, or whatever his work might be, and followed instantly.

The significant thing to remember is His amazing faith in plain ordinary folk. He did not look over the Blue Book or the Directory of Directories, saying to Himself, "This is the most important mission that any one ever undertook; I must have the very best and ablest assistants." On the contrary, it was almost as though He said, "If I can pick up about a dozen honest chaps who are physically strong enough to stand hardships and simple enough to let their faith carry them beyond intellectual doubts, I can trust this message of mine to their keeping and feel sure that it will never die out." That supreme confidence in common humanity sets Him apart from most other leaders who have attempted large things, and the magnificent way in which His faith was justified is one of the finest proofs of His divinity.

It will be worth while to look briefly at these pupils of His. How many of us know anything at all about them, or could even write a list of their names? The first two of the permanent disciples were John, the son of Zebedee (with whom was afterward associated his brother, James), and Andrew. Andrew was apparently the sort of man who likes to discover good things and then tell them to a brother or to some one else with more initiative than himself. That is the fate of many of the world's most useful characters. He had been with Jesus only about an hour when he slipped away and brought his brother Simon. Almost at once Simon began to achieve a degree of prominence which Andrew could never have attained. Andrew accepted the situation loyally and so far as we know was never jealous of his more emphatic and outspoken brother, though he might have thought he had good reason for being. The next day Jesus found another Galilean named Philip, who also had a friend, Nathanael. These are the first six—

John and James.
Andrew and Simon.
Philip and Nathanael.
All play important parts.

Then came two others who never were prominent: James, the son of Alphæus, and Thaddæus whose other name was Lebbæus. Finally there were four more, each of whom was important and is known by name to all of us. Levi, or Matthew, was a tax-gatherer whom Jesus called "as He passed by." Whether Matthew went through any ceremony of repentance and baptism is not recorded, but we are told that he made a great feast to which pretty much the whole town was invited. It was because of His attendance at such feasts, with their indiscriminate guest lists, that Jesus was criticized as a "wine bibber" and a "gluttonous man." To such criticism He responded with some of the noblest of His parables, the Lost Sheep, the Lost Coin and, best of all, the Prodigal Son.

The tenth in our list is Thomas, a moody fellow who insisted on thinking things out for himself. "Doubting Thomas" he has been called because after the resurrection, when some of the disciples claimed to have seen Jesus, Thomas answered stoutly:

> Except I shall see in his hands the print of the nails, and put my finger into the print of the nails, and thrust my hand into his side, I will not believe.

It is unfair to Thomas to remember only his doubt and to forget that when the disciples were trying to dissuade Jesus from His last dangerous journey to Jerusalem it was this same Thomas who exclaimed, "Let us also go, that we may die with him."

There was as number eleven another Simon, whose surname, "the zealot," does not mean that he personally was of an over-zealous disposition but that he had been a participant in one of the sporadic revolutions against Roman authority. You might term him a socialist if you wanted a not very exact but sufficiently convenient description. And finally there was Judas, the only one of the twelve who was not a Galilean but who, as a member of the royal tribe of Judah, felt himself superior to the crowd of fishermen, publicans and common folk. Better educated than the rest, a man of business ability, he was treasurer and "carried the bag." When Jesus said, "Take no thought for the morrow, saying, what shall we eat or what shall we drink," it may have sounded all right to the other eleven, but you can imagine the look of mingled cynicism and worry on the face of Judas who had to pay the bills. Equipped by talent and training to be of larger service than any of the others, he was the only traitor.

These, then, were the "twelve" who were destined to change human history.

The public life of Jesus appears to have covered just three years: a year of organization and small beginnings; a year of dramatic deeds and great successes; a year of diminishing popularity and disappointments. He started quietly in the little towns near His home, talking to whomever would listen and taking advantage of any occasion that brought people together. There was a marriage in the neighboring village of Cana, and He was invited with His mother. At a critical moment in the celebration Mary caught a look of distress in the eyes of the hostess and with quick feminine instinct divined the situation. The wine had given out. There occurred then the first miracle of Jesus, the transforming of water into wine. Very few sermons are preached about this miracle, and it is usually glossed over as being not quite in keeping with the character of His life and work. But to those of us who picture Him as the Great Companion, sociable, loving crowds, followed everywhere by bands of laughing children, this beginning of His public activity seems splendidly significant. Only a few weeks before He had refused to employ His miraculous power to turn stones into bread to satisfy His own hunger; He had not yet employed it to heal the sick or convey a moral lesson. But He did not think it beneath the dignity of His mission to perform a miracle in order that the happiness of a company of friendly folk might be continued and a hostess preserved from embarrassment.

In Capernaum, which was another near-by place, He healed sick people and attracted crowds by His preaching so that His reputation spread and there were rumors about Him even in Jerusalem, the capital. His entrance into that city was dramatic and lifted Him instantly out of the class of ordinary country philosophers and made Him a national character. It was in the outer court of the Temple, the center of the religious life of the nation, a spot that ought to have been more holy than any other but which had been degraded by greed into a noisome market-place. He

> found in the temple those that sold oxen and sheep and doves, and the changers of money sitting:
> And when he had made a scourge of small cords, he drove them all out of the temple, and the sheep, and the oxen; and poured out the changers' money, and overthrew the tables;
> And said unto them that sold doves, Take these things hence; make not my Father's house an house of merchandise.

That night His name was on every tongue; His great success had begun.

Immense crowds flocked about Him. Once He had to push out into the lake in a little boat, using it as a pulpit. Again He sat them down upon the green slopes of a mountain and there delivered the one long discourse of His ministry, a talk which contains many of the most sublime thoughts ever put into human language.

> Blessed are the poor in spirit; for theirs is the kingdom of heaven. . . .
> Blessed are the merciful; for they shall obtain mercy.
> Blessed are the pure in heart: for they shall see God. . . .
> Ye have heard that it hath been said, Thou shalt love thy neighbour, and hate thine enemy.
> But I say unto you, Love your enemies, bless

them that curse you, do good to them that hate
you, and pray for them that despitefully use you,
and persecute you;

That ye may be the children of your Father
which is in heaven: for he maketh the sun to rise
upon the evil and on the good, and sendeth rain on
the just and on the unjust. . . .

Lay not up for yourselves treasures upon earth,
where moth and rust doth corrupt, and where
thieves break through and steal:

But lay up for yourselves treasures in
heaven . . .

For where your treasure is, there will your heart
be also. . . .

Behold the fowls of the air: for they sow not,
neither do they reap, nor gather into barns; yet
your heavenly Father feedeth them. Are ye not
much better than they?

Which of you by taking thought can add one
cubit unto his stature?

And why take ye thought for raiment? Consider the lilies of the field, how they grow; they
toil not, neither do they spin:

And yet I say unto you that even Solomon in
all his glory was not arrayed like one of these.

Wherefore, if God so clothe the grass of the
field, which to day is, and to morrow is cast into
the oven, shall he not much more clothe you, O ye
of little faith?

His miracles caused His reputation to spread
before Him, and the most dramatic of them,
the feeding of a host of people, was followed by
one great moment of triumph, which, however,

marked the beginning of the end. That multitude of people whom He had seated in groups of fifty and a hundred rose to their feet after their miraculous meal and discovered that they were an army. They looked up with new eyes at the strong young man who had fed them as Moses had fed their ancestors in the wilderness. The words of the prophets surged into their minds. Here indeed was a son of David; here was the promised leader who should free his people, drive the Romans before him, and sit again upon the throne in Jerusalem. With a great shout they surged forward.

Did He hesitate for a moment? Was there an instant in which the temptation to seize this proffered leadership battled with His real ideals? We know only the final decision, which was quickly made:

> When Jesus therefore perceived that they would come and take him by force, to make him a king, *he departed again into a mountain himself alone.*

From that hour His popularity waned. Most of those who had followed Him in the hope of reward through a successful revolution began to drop away.

> From that time many of his disciples went back, and walked no more with him.

Even the twelve were disappointed and disheartened. Why was it necessary for Him to be so inflexible? Why must He always abuse the Pharisees and other influential people? Why turn away so abruptly from those who could be of so much help? Jesus alone saw clearly. He led them away from Galilee into the foreign shores of Tyre and Sidon. He wanted to be alone with them, to try to make them understand why He must refuse temporal power; why, indeed, it would be necessary for Him to insure the permanency of His message by sealing it with His blood. He must "go into Jerusalem," He told them, "and suffer many things of the elders and chief priests and scribes, and be killed." Indignantly they sought to dissuade him. "Be it far from thee, Lord," the hot-headed Peter exclaimed, "this shall never be unto thee." Their remonstrances were in vain. Quietly, courageously. He turned about and prepared for the journey to Jerusalem which would be the end.

The whole last year of His ministry has a different tone. He is far more emphatic, far more audacious. Knowing that compromise is useless, He lashes out against the smug complacency of the Pharisees who render lip service to Jehovah but are rotten at the core with selfishness and greed. He knew what Fate held in store for Him; the warnings had been coming in quick succession for more than a year. The death of John the Baptist was the first one. Cast into prison for denouncing the licentious marriage of Herod, John was sacrificed to the wicked request of the wife, Herodias, and her abandoned daughter, Salome.

> And when the daughter of the said Herodias came in, and danced, and pleased Herod and them that sat with him, the king said unto the damsel, Ask of me whatsoever thou wilt and I will give it thee. . . .
> And she went forth, and said unto her mother, What shall I ask? And she said, The head of John the Baptist. . . .
> And immediately the king sent an executioner . . .
> And brought his head in a charger, and gave it to the damsel: and the damsel gave it to her mother.

The death of John cast a permanent shadow over the heart of Jesus and added greatly to the force and bitterness of His denunciations. His rejection by His home town, Nazareth, was another blow. It is easy to imagine the high hopes with which He had turned His steps toward it. He had already succeeded in Capernaum and near-by cities; He had made a great stir in the capital. For the first time in history the name of Nazareth was linked with the name of a national character. He would go back to His old friends and neighbors, give them the glad tidings, heal their sick, and share with them the joys of success. But the town received Him scornfully. "You may have fooled them in Capernaum," the cynical faces said, "but little old Nazareth isn't so slow. You're no prophet; we know you. You're just the boy who used to work in the carpenter shop."

> He could do there no mighty work because of their unbelief.

His mother and brothers wavered, feeling it unsafe to be closely connected with one who was stirring up so much opposition. They urged Him to go up to Jerusalem.

> For even his brethren did not believe in him.

So, deserted by those who ought to have stood by Him most staunchly, abandoned by this popular following, supported only by His original little group of disciples, and they wavering and in doubt, He made His way back to Jerusalem to face the events of that last great week which the Gospels give us in such full detail. In the final hour of tragedy even His disciples were missing. Only a few stricken women huddled at the foot of the Cross, and the last word of faith was spoken not by a friend but fell from the lips of a crucified thief:

> Lord, remember me when thou comest into thy kingdom.

So He died, and those who had demanded His blood regarded their triumph as complete. Surely a little group of unlettered peasants could do nothing without leadership. Jerusalem and the Roman power would now be safe from the menace of one who gave common people the foolish idea that they were sons of God and, hence, the equals of the king. What actually happened is set forth with force and conviction in each of the four Gospels, separately. His disciples declared that He still lived. On their report the tomb was examined and found empty. In the city where He had been put to death disciples set to work with results so immediate and astonishing that even the Roman authorities were shortly compelled to take notice. They began to produce a literature, and with this we shall deal in the next chapter.

The pious men who broke the Bible up into chapters and numbered verses contributed something to our convenience but they destroyed the swing and charm of the unbroken narrative.

THE BOOK NOBODY KNOWS

The Scriptures are fed to us in Sunday-school in measured doses of about eight verses a week; we read the Bible, when we read it at all, one or two chapters a day. This is not our habit with other thrilling literature; we give a good story a real chance by reading it straight through in a single interested sitting. Try this plan some day with the book of Luke and follow it with the Acts. Forget that you have ever seen the Bible before; read the whole account of the great beginnings as you would read any other finely told chapter of history. See if it is not indeed an invigorating experience.

It is the story that changed the whole world. In saying that we are not unmindful of the limitations of the work of Jesus. He did not overthrow the oppressive government of Rome. He did not lower the tax rate. He did not improve sanitary conditions in Jerusalem, nor erect a public library at Nazareth. He did not increase the wages of Christians over those of infidels. He taught no sure cure for disease. The economic status of His followers was exactly as it had been; He found them fishermen, He left them fishermen. He did nothing to justify those who talk as though the "economic interpretation of history" were the last word in wisdom.

128

THE GREAT LIFE

But His fishermen were different fishermen, transformed, endowed with power, capable of great faith and magnificent achievement. Through them and their successors He started more philanthropies than all men who have ever lived. Hospitals and clinics, charities and libraries, schools and colleges, have multiplied where He has inspired the souls of men. His religion is the best asset of civilization. That part of the world outside of which very few of us would willingly spend our days is named for Him, Christendom.

IV
THE ACTS AND THE EPISTLES

QUESTIONS

1. *What lie made Ananias eternally notorious?*
   Acts 5:1-11.
2. *What was the first name of Christianity?*
   Answered in this chapter.
3. *Where was the term Christians first employed?*
   Acts 11:26.
4. *What created the need for it?*
   Answered in this chapter.
5. *What caused the first heresy trial in the history*
   of the church?
   Acts 15:1-12.
6. *How was it settled?*
   Acts 15:13-29.
7. *Who became a convert to Christianity after being*
   soundly thrashed?
   Acts 18:17; I Cor. 1:1.
8. *What reception did Paul meet in Athens?*
   Acts 17:17-33.
9. *How can you distinguish in reading The Acts,*
   from chapter 16 to the end, between what
   Luke actually saw and how much he heard
   from other witnesses?
   Answered in this chapter.
10. *Where was the New Testament begun?*
    Answered in this chapter.

IV

THE ACTS AND THE EPISTLES

THE peril of building up an organization around a single person is that when he dies or withdraws the organization falls to pieces. "An institution is the lengthened shadow of a man," but there have been many men eminent in their day who cast no such shadow. The good they did, as Marc Antony said, is oft interred with their bones. Surely this process of disintegration, natural enough following the death of any leader, would be inevitable when The Leader had died a felon's death and the followers were unlettered peasants. The authorities at Jerusalem took this complacent point of view and rested easy.

They received a rude shock within a very few days. Peter and John, in preaching on the streets of the city and performing deeds of healing, gathered crowds that interfered with traffic and caused them to be arrested. Thinking to overawe these simple fellows, the High Priest Annas and his colleagues presided per-

sonally at the trial. Picture their amazement
when Peter broke into vigorous denunciation of
them as the murderers of the Lord in whose
name only salvation could be found.

> Now when they saw the *boldness* of Peter and
> John, . . . they marvelled; and they took
> knowledge of them, that they had been with Jesus.

Those words deserve notice for the light they
throw upon the figure and manner of the real
Jesus as contrasted with the unsatisfying por-
traits of Him that have come down to us through
the ages. Painters have painted Him and writers
have written about Him as a "man of sorrows,"
a physical weakling, a "lamb," an unhappy man
who was disappointed and glad to die. The
conquering attitude of the disciples does not
tally with such descriptions. The Bible does not
say of them, "seeing the lamb-like character of
Peter and John" or "seeing that Peter and John
were men of sorrow and acquainted with grief,"
but "seeing the *boldness* of Peter and John" the
authorities knew that such men must have been
the friends and companions of Jesus.

So characteristic was this boldness, so vigorous were the disciples in the propagation of the
faith, that within less than twenty years the
rulers of the far removed city of Thessalonica
were troubled by the report that

THE ACTS AND THE EPISTLES

These that have turned the world upside down are come hither also; . . . and these all do contrary to the decrees of Cæsar, saying that there is another king, one Jesus.

Only a little later, not more than forty years after the death of St. Paul, Pliny the Roman Governor of Bithynia is compelled to write to the Emperor Trajan for instructions as to how he may check the growth of this extraordinary new sect. Since his letter and Trajan's reply are the only genuinely ancient records outside of the Bible itself which bear directly upon early apostolic activities, they are worth quoting at some length:

To the Emperor Trajan: It is my invariable rule, Sir, to refer to you in all matters where I feel doubtful; for who is more capable of removing my scruples, or informing my ignorance? Having never been present at any trials concerning those who profess Christianity, I am unacquainted not only with the nature of their crimes, or the measure of their punishment, but how far it is proper to enter into an examination concerning them. Whether, therefore, any difference is usually made with respect to ages, or no distinction is to be observed between the young and the adult; whether repentance entitles them to a pardon; or if a man has been once a Christian, it avails nothing to desist from his error; whether the very profession of Christianity, unattended with any criminal act, or only the crimes themselves inherent in the profession are punishable; on all these points I am in great doubt. In the meanwhile, the method I have observed towards those who have been brought before me as Christians is this: I asked them whether they were Christians; if they admitted it, I repeated the question twice, and threatened them with punishment; if they persisted, I ordered them to be at once punished: for I was persuaded, whatever the nature of their opinions might be, a contumacious and inflexible obstinacy certainly deserved correction. . . .

This contagious superstition is not confined to the cities only, but has spread its infection among the neighbouring villages and country. Nevertheless, it still seems possible to restrain its progress. The temples, at least, which were once almost deserted, begin now to be frequented; and the sacred rites, after a long intermission, are again revived; while there is a general demand for the victims, which till lately found very few purchasers. From all this it is easy to conjecture what numbers might be reclaimed if a general pardon were granted to those who shall repent of their error.

Trajan to Pliny: You have adopted the right course, my dearest Secundus, in investigating the charges against the Christians who were brought before you. It is not possible to lay down any general rule for all such cases. Do not go out of your way to look for them. If indeed they should be brought before you, and the crime is proved, they must be punished; with the restriction, however, that where the party denies he is a Christian and shall make it evident that he is not, by invoking our gods, let him (notwithstanding any former suspicion) be pardoned upon his repentance. Anonymous informations ought not to be received in any sort of prosecution. It is introducing a very dangerous precedent, and is quite foreign to the spirit of our age.

So rapidly has the shadow of the Cross extended that in less than a single century it falls across the emperor's throne. Let us turn back to the Bible record and trace the dramatic steps by which this incredible success was won.

The book of the Acts of the Apostles opens significantly:

The former treatise have I made, O Theophilus, of all that Jesus *began* both to do and to teach.

That sentence tells us first that the book was written by the same man who wrote the Book of Luke and to the same man, Theophilus; and, second, that the writer, in common with the other disciples, regarded the three brief years of Jesus' public work as merely the beginning of His larger life and influence. So the events proved.

Jerusalem of those days was a populous and crowded city, and the disciples were countrymen from an outlying province. Yet, after a brief period of bewilderment, they organized themselves and became immediately a center of power. Thousands of men, some of them prominent in the city's life, came out to their meetings, confessed to the crime that had been done in the murder of Jesus, and became his truest followers.

Jesus and the original twelve had pooled their revenues in the "bag" which Judas carried, and he had paid all the expenses. For a time the Jerusalem community attempted to operate on this basis and, while there was no hard and fast rule, the sentiment was in favor of a common purse, and most of the group acceded to it. This led to the first tragedy.

A man named Ananias and his wife Sapphira wanted credit for having given their all, but they kept back half of the price of the land they had sold. Peter called Ananias to account, and he brazenly repeated his lie. Peter looked hard at him and said:

> Ananias, why hath Satan filled thine heart to lie to the Holy Ghost, and to keep back part of the price of the land?
> Whilst it remained, was it not thine own? and after it was sold, was it not in thine own power? why hast thou conceived this thing in thine heart? thou hast not lied unto men but unto God.
> And Ananias hearing these words fell down, and

gave up the ghost: and great fear came on all
them that heard these things.

And the young men arose, wound him up, and
carried him out, and buried him.

Three hours later Sapphira came in and repeated
the lie and met a similar fate. The incident profoundly impressed the young community. It
appears from the narrative that the disciples
were not required to give up their property and
that some of them did not do so and suffered
no reproach. But the sham of pretending to do
so met with tragic rebuke. Communism failed
even under the most sacredly favorable circumstances and probably always will fail short of
the millennium. The fact that it was attempted
at all, however, indicates the earnest idealism of
that early group and helps to explain the spirit
which carried their faith to the ends of the world
and laid the strong foundations of the church.

The Jews of that period were widely scattered. They had large families and a small
country. There were colonies in almost every
important city in the Mediterranean section, but
they had times of home-coming at the several
annual feasts in Jerusalem. The disciples took
advantage of these occasions to preach to crowds
that came from widely scattered places, and so
quite early there began to be followers of Jesus,

not only throughout Palestine but in Egypt and as far north as Antioch. It was in Antioch that need was first discovered for a name that should distinguish between ordinary Jews and the Jews that recognized the leadership of Jesus, and "the disciples were first called Christians at Antioch." Up to that time the followers of Jesus had simply spoken of themselves as of "the Way." The first name of Christianity was "the Road."

In all these early movements Peter was the foremost figure. He developed a gift of speech that surprised his friends, and he never lacked courage. But presently there came on the stage a new figure of vast influence. One of the early preachers, Stephen, had given especial attention to those Christians in Jerusalem who had not been born Jews but had come in as proselytes. He was arrested and condemned to death, and was executed by stoning. Doubtless the people who did the actual throwing of the stones were for the most part of the rabble, but "a young man named Saul," a zealous Pharisee, looked on with approval at a sentence which he as a member of the Sanhedrin, or high court, had helped to pass. Those who threw the stones

laid down their clothes at a young man's feet, whose name was Saul.

This young man named Saul was an ardent persecutor. He heard that the Christian faith was spreading as far as Damascus and he obtained letters to the Jewish authorities there for the arrest of any who were of "the Way." He left Jerusalem very eager to carry out his errand, but with a growing inward uneasiness. He was mentally "kicking against the pricks" or goads of his own conscience. He remembered Stephen, whose face during his trial and execution had been "like the face of an angel." Riding along the road toward Damascus at midday, which is not a good time for a man to be riding there, he was stricken down by what may have been sunstroke: but with it came, as he believed, a voice, saying, "Saul, Saul, why persecutest thou me?" Saul's companions saw the blinding light but did not hear the voice. Saul asked, "Who art thou, Lord?" And again the voice came, "I am Jesus whom thou persecutest."

Saul's conversion was instantaneous, yet its development was most interesting. Instead of arresting any one in Damascus, he at once announced his change of convictions, and had to escape from the city by means of a basket let down from the wall. For three years he retired to Arabia. When he emerged he had a definite plan. He would go back to Jerusalem to be welcomed by the disciples, who would naturally choose him as their leader, and so he would become minister of the First Church in Jerusalem. It was a grand plan, but it met with bitter disappointment. When he arrived in Jerusalem the disciples were afraid of him and, even after he had been vouched for by Barnabas, gave him a very grudging welcome.

Rebuffed but still ardent, he went to his old home in Tarsus, a Greek city, where he had been born, a Jew but with full right of Roman citizenship, a fact of which he was immensely proud and of which he took full advantage. For a while he had little to do. Then Barnabas, a discoverer of men greater than himself, the discoverer of Mark, went to Tarsus and invited Saul to come to Antioch where the work was making great progress. Saul went, and a new chapter in the ethical and spiritual history of the world began there.

After a very successful work in Antioch, Barnabas and Saul proposed to visit the old home of Barnabas in the island of Cyprus, and to preach as they went. This they did, and took with them Mark, who was a nephew of Barnabas. In Cyprus they had great success and established a friendship with the Roman governor, Sergius Paulus. Saul, named for the Old Testament

king, now changed his name to Paulus, probably
after this governor. From Cyprus they went
into the nearer regions of Asia Minor.

And now an occasion of irritation arose.
Barnabas was the leader of this journey, but
Saul everywhere became the more prominent
character. Barnabas was evidently a tall impressive man; Paul much smaller, more active,
and nervous. In one place on the mainland they
were received with such honor that there was
a proposal to deify them:

> And they called Barnabas, Jupiter; and Paul,
> Mercurius, because he was the chief speaker.

Mark did not like the way things were going.
His uncle Barnabas was the really great man,
but Paul was taking the lion's share of the
honors. Mark made himself disagreeable, and
Paul did not like Mark, who finally left the two
older men and went back to Jerusalem. In due
time Paul and Barnabas followed, and both at
Antioch and later at Jerusalem gave a vivid
account of a most successful tour.

Thus far there had been no serious quarrel in
the church, but the calm was about to be broken.
Barnabas and Paul had found that others than
Jews were eager to know about Jesus, and the
question was whether these people in becoming

converts must become Jewish proselytes. Barnabas saw no reason why Christianity should be a mere sect of Judaism, and Paul was emphatic in the same opinion. But the older disciples, all Jews, could not see how a man could be a Christian and not keep the whole Old Testament law.

A strange thing had happened at Jerusalem. The brothers of Jesus had not believed in Him during His ministry, and at one time thought Him insane, but after His death they became loyal converts. Two of them, Jude and James, wrote short books, which are in the New Testament, and James went to Jerusalem and became very active in the church there. He was a "just man," a phrase that had been used of his father Joseph, and was a very devout student of the Old Testament law. It is said that his knees became calloused like those of a camel through his long periods of prayer. He was the head of the conservative faction, and Peter was at first of the same persuasion. James, by reason of his brotherhood to Jesus, had risen above Peter in Jerusalem, and he it was who presided over the first heresy trial in church history—the trial of Paul and Barnabas for baptizing Gentiles without insisting that they conform to the whole Jewish ritual.

It was a decidedly surprising experience for Paul. He had sat in Jerusalem as one of the seventy members of the Sanhedrin, the supreme court of the nation. Now he found himself back in the same city before Peter and James and John in positions not unlike that which he had occupied. He saw "those that were reputed to be somebody," as he rather loftily described them, and said, "whatsoever they were it maketh no matter to me"; and declared that they got more from him than he had ever got from them, that he neither went out under their authority nor recognized their right to tell him what he should preach. All the same, he cared greatly for their good-will and the effect of their endorsement.

The story is told in the fifteenth chapter of Acts, one of the great documents in the history of the liberation of the human spirit. Paul's accusers presented their case, and Paul and Barnabas replied, and after a long debate a compromise was arrived at. The church in Jerusalem, consisting entirely of Jews, would stand firm for the old fundamentals, but the churches abroad, being Gentile, might follow a more liberal faith. At the suggestion of James a letter was sent out to the Gentile brethren in the churches which Paul had organized:

> Forasmuch as we have heard, that certain which went out from us have troubled you with words subverting your souls, saying, Ye must be circumcised, and keep the law: to whom we gave no such commandment: . . .
>
> For it seemed good to the Holy Ghost, and to us, to lay upon you no greater burden than these necessary things;
>
> That ye abstain from meats offered to idols, and from blood, and from things strangled, and from fornication: from which if ye keep yourselves, ye shall do well. Fare ye well.

Thus there were to be two kinds of Christianity, the fundamentalist and the liberal, and they were not to quarrel. Christians who had been reared as Jews were to be required to keep the whole Mosaic law, and those who were not so reared were to be accepted on their love of Jesus and a very simple code of morality. Paul left Jerusalem jubilant. He had won out. Telling later about "those who would have taken away our liberties," he says,

> To whom we gave place by subjection, no, not for an hour; that the truth of the gospel might continue with you.

Paul was a doughty fighter and he had good need to be.

He and Barnabas were now ready to start on another missionary journey and a longer one.

But they had a quarrel. Paul would not go if Mark went along, and Barnabas would not leave Mark behind.

> And the contention was so sharp between them, that they departed asunder one from the other: and so Barnabas took Mark, and sailed unto Cyprus;
> And Paul chose Silas, and departed, being recommended by the brethren unto the grace of God.

Paul did not get on very well. He met a series of hindrances and changed his route several times. At length he came to Troas, the site of ancient Troy, where he fell ill and saw in a vision a man of Macedonia, saying, "Come over into Macedonia and help us." Read carefully the next sentence (Acts 16:10); it is notable for its pronouns:

> And after *he* had seen the vision, immediately *we* endeavoured to go into Macedonia.

Where do we get this *we?* Who were the *we?*

Paul was one of them, but he is not the writer. Silas and Timothy were two others, but they are not the writers.

Who is it that comes into the narrative just at this point, under the shelter of this little word "we"? It is the physician-author, Doctor Luke.

From here on the book of Acts is made up of two kinds of material, that which says "we" and that which says "he" or "they." The "we" sections show the times when Luke was present; the rest of the story he got from others. You will find it interesting to read the book of Acts from chapter sixteen to the end and discover just how much Luke actually saw and how much he heard from witnesses.

And now the good news took on a new character. Paul had crossed into Europe and found a fresh field. He preached in Philippi, in Thessalonica, which is modern Salonica, in Berea, and even in proud Athens. That sophisticated city was the capital of the smart world.

> For all the Athenians and strangers which were there spent their time in nothing else, but either to tell, or to hear some new thing.

Partly out of curiosity, partly from genuine intellectual interest, the Athenians allowed Paul to make his way up to Mars Hill and there set forth this new religion of which he was the representative. It was a keen test of his mental agility and he met it nobly.

> Ye men of Athens [he began], I perceive that in all things ye are very religious. [Nothing in that to give offense.]

148

For as I passed by, and beheld your devotions, I found an altar with this inscription, TO THE UNKNOWN GOD. Whom therefore ye ignorantly worship, him declare I unto you.

A magnificent flank attack. Sophisticated and cynical as they were, he had piqued their curiosity. They must hear about this unknown God or run the risk of missing some important "new thing," so they stood quietly and allowed him to finish, while

some mocked: and others said, We will hear thee again of this matter.

From Athens Paul went to Corinth, then the Panama of the ancient world where a boom was in progress waiting a government appropriation for the digging of the canal, which had still to wait seventeen hundred years. Bachelor as he was, Paul utilized more than any of the other apostles the abilities of women. In Corinth he was fortunate in finding a woman of talent, Priscilla, who with her husband, Aquila, took him in. He and they were tent-makers and worked together; and Paul soon began to gather converts. The orthodox ruler of the synagogue, Sosthenes, did not like the way things were going and stirred up a crowd which hurried Paul before the Roman deputy, with the characteristically intolerant charge:

> This fellow persuadeth men to worship God contrary to the law.

The deputy, Gallio, was brother to the philosopher Seneca and a man of solid common sense.

> And when Paul was now about to open his mouth, Gallio said unto the Jews, If it were a matter of wrong or wicked lewdness, O ye Jews, reason would that I should bear with you:
> But if it be a question of words and names, and of your law; look ye to it; for I will be no judge of such matters.
> And he drave them from the judgment seat.

With characteristic fickleness the crowd now turned on Sosthenes and administered a sound beating, which was in process when Gallio stepped out of the court room:

> And Gallio cared for none of those things.

Paul, who had been beaten repeatedly and once stoned and left for dead, rather enjoyed the spectacle, and the thrashing did Sosthenes good, for he subsequently became a convert. Indeed, when Paul was at Ephesus a few years later Sosthenes was with him and appears in the en-

viable position of joint author of the letter to
the home folk, the Corinthians:

> Paul, called to be an apostle of Jesus Christ
> through the will of God, and Sosthenes our
> brother,
> Unto the church of God which is at Corinth.

Sometimes it takes a sound beating to open a
hard-shelled mind to new truth, and the subsequent results may be of great benefit.

It was in Corinth that Paul developed what
came to be his method: simply to move along
the Roman roads from city to city, selecting
important and favorable centers and "digging
in" for a stay of considerable length, and establishing a work that would radiate in different
directions through the agency of his own helpers
and such visitors as came to see him and took
away with them the essentials of his message.

But another thing happened in Corinth in
that autumn, a momentous thing. *There the
New Testament began to be written.*

We have already considered the writing of
the four gospels. The date of the first of them,
Mark, is about 61, and Paul reached Corinth
ten years earlier, in 51. Up to that time the
story of the life of Jesus had been told orally.
No one felt the need of a written biography; no

one felt qualified to write it. So it was not with the gospels that the actual writing of the New Testament began, but with the letter which Paul in Corinth wrote to his old church in Thessalonica, the Epistle to the Thessalonians. You will be interested in the story.

Go back to the period before Paul's arrival in Corinth, to his crossing from old Troy to Europe. He had seen a vision of a man of Macedonia inviting him into Europe, and he went. The little boat that carried him and his three companions, Timothy, Silas and Luke, bore the most precious freight that ever landed on the western shore of the Mediterranean. But Paul did not meet the man of Macedonia. For a good while he had a hard time. As we have already noted, he was beaten and imprisoned in Philippi, mobbed in Thessalonica, driven out of town from Berea, and flouted in Athens. "Our flesh had no rest," he wrote about those days. "Without were fightings and within were fears." When he arrived in Corinth he was alone, having left Silas at Berea, and Timothy at Thessalonica.

The weeks while he waited for them to come to him were a period in which Paul was very near to nervous prostration. If it had not been for Priscilla's good cooking and the companion-

ship which he found with her and her husband,
he might have broken down entirely. His whole
work since coming to Europe seemed a total
failure; it had brought only hardship and humiliation.

He was afraid Timothy and Silas would never
come. He was afraid they would be mobbed to
death. And if they came he feared they would
say: "It's no use. These people just will not
hear the good news. In Philippi they say that
if they had us back in jail we would never get
out. In Berea they are ready to quote the
Jewish law against us and say that Jesus did not
measure up to the prophecies. In Thessalonica
we dared not go on the streets in daylight. In
Athens your sermon is a joke."

So in his lonesomeness he conjectured and
was tortured by his imagination. But one day
two dusty travelers arrived in Corinth, found
the Ghetto, and there inquired if a man was
boarding somewhere in town, a small, wiry,
nervous man of defective sight, named Paul.
To their joy they learned that he was staying
with Aquila and Priscilla; they hunted him up,
and there was a glad reunion. Paul could
hardly restrain himself.

"How is the work going?" we can imagine
him asking.

"Fine," cried Timothy and Silas.

"You mean in Philippi?"

"Yes, there and everywhere else."

"In Berea?"

"Yes, the church is growing every day."

"But surely not in Thessalonica?"

"Yes, in Thessalonica, too. And they remember you with gratitude and want you to come back."

Paul was almost intoxicated with joy. The heartbreaking anxiety found relief in an ecstasy of satisfaction. The work was going well everywhere, even in Thessalonica! And they hoped he would come back! Eagerly he called for parchment and, with Timothy as a volunteer stenographer, he dictated a letter to send back to Thessalonica.

He told them how he had left with his two companions, but on reaching Athens had changed his mind and sent Silas and Timothy back:

Wherefore when we could no longer forbear, we thought it good to be left at Athens alone;

And sent Timotheus, our brother, and minister of God, and our fellow-labourer in the gospel of Christ, to establish you.

It almost killed him to think that they might have forsaken their faith. But they had not; they were standing fast.

But when Timotheus came from you unto us,
and brought us good tidings of your faith and
charity, and that ye have good remembrance of
us always, desiring greatly to see us, as we also
to see you:
Therefore, brethren, we are comforted over you
in all our affliction and distress by your faith:
For now we live, if ye stand fast in the Lord.

So he dictated, fast as Timothy could write,
and sent the letter by a messenger going north
from Corinth. He put in sundry exhortations,
a little doctrinal teaching, and started the message forth on its eventful journey. He did not
know that he had begun a new Bible. He never
suspected that this impetuously composed first
letter to the Thessalonians was to be the first
volume in a new sacred library. But it was;
and that is the way the New Testament began.

He had to write a second letter to the Thessalonians to answer some questions growing out
of the first one. These letters were lent to
near-by churches and copied and read to the con-
gregations. Paul heard how widely they were
used and so he wrote more and more. He had
learned to supplement the living voice with the
written page. If he were at work to-day he
would not only preach; he would be a regular
contributor to the press. He would love the
smell of printers' ink.

After eighteen months in Corinth he went back to Jerusalem and gave account of his second missionary journey. He had a string of new churches through Asia Minor, Macedonia and Greece. He had developed his method, and he was happy in the knowledge of a great success. He remained in Palestine only a few months; it had grown too small for him. But while he was there he wrote one letter that must have attention. He learned that in Galatia, in Asia Minor, where he had established churches, he had been followed by fundamentalists who were telling the people that Paul was not really an apostle; that he possessed no real authority; that the good news as he had taught it was defective because he did not teach the Mosaic law.

Now Paul had great respect for the Mosaic law, and he did not object to the fundamentalists provided they kept on their own side. But to have them invading a field which he had developed and to start a divisive doctrine there, looking not forward but back, was too much for his hot temper and strong conviction. At once he called for his trusty pen and after the formal greeting he plunged straight into his message:

> I marvel that ye are so soon removed from him that called you into the grace of Christ unto another Gospel:

156

> Which is not another; but there be some that
> trouble you, and would pervert the gospel of
> Christ.
>
> But though we, or an angel from heaven, preach
> any other gospel unto you than that which we
> have preached unto you, let him be ac-
> cursed. . . .
>
> For do I now persuade men, or God? or do I
> seek to please men? for if I yet pleased men, I
> should not be the servant of Christ.
>
> But I certify you, brethren, that the gospel
> which was preached of me is not after man.

He goes on to remind them of his history—how
he was the chief persecutor of the church, but,
being converted, received his message not from
the group in Jerusalem but from God direct, in
his hours of quiet retreat in Arabia. He went
to Jerusalem, he says, and met with James, "the
Lord's brother," and he and Peter agreed concerning the right of Gentiles to be received into
communion without being compelled to comply
with the Mosaic law, and he won his fight.
When later, at Antioch, Peter backslid into the
old hard-shell theology, Paul had refuted him
openly.

> But when Peter was come to Antioch, I with-
> stood him to the face, because he was to be blamed.

By subsequent battles and by many persecutions, of which he bore the scars, he had won the

right of his churches to freedom. Were they now proposing to abandon this great freedom because some strict constructionists from Judea came among them, stirring up trouble?

> Stand fast therefore in the liberty wherewith Christ hath made us free, and be not entangled again with the yoke of bondage. . . .
> For all the law is fulfilled in one word, even in this: Thou shalt love thy neighbor as thyself. . . .
> If we live in the Spirit, let us also walk in the Spirit.
> Let us not be desirous of vain glory, provoking one another, enjoying one another. . . .
> Be not deceived; God is not mocked; for whatsoever a man soweth, that shall he also reap.
> For he that soweth to his flesh shall of the flesh reap corruption; but he that soweth to the Spirit shall of the Spirit reap life everlasting.
> And let us not be weary in well doing: for in due season we shall reap, if we faint not.

That white-hot letter to the Galatians, product of intense moral indignation, whose curses remain untranslated because the translators have feared to put them into plain English, is the Magna Charta of Christian liberty. It is the rebuke of bigotry and the battle cry of freedom.

Paul soon set forth on his third and last missionary journey. He started northward as he had done before, passing from Antioch by land around the end of the Mediterranean, preaching as he went, till he came to Ephesus. There he seemed to find an opening in the Jewish synagogue, but after three months a sharp clash arose, and he rented a schoolroom from a philosopher named Tyrannus, the philosopher using it half a day and Paul the other half. He took a two years' lease of this place and developed his extension service so fully

> that all they which dwelt in Asia [the province, not the continent] heard the word of the Lord Jesus, both Jews and Greeks.

The growth of his body of adherents was so remarkable that in this city, where the beautiful temple of Diana stood, and her shrine was sacred, the idol makers were almost out of work. A large mass meeting of the silversmiths and allied trades convened in the theater. There was a great shout for two hours, "Great is Diana of the Ephesians." But then, as often,

> the more part knew not wherefore they were come together.

So the crowd shouted itself tired without violence, and the town clerk said a tactful word that dismissed the assembly.

In Ephesus, before this riot made his withdrawal wise, Paul heard occasionally from his churches in Macedonia and Achaia, and he kept in touch with them by means of his letters, which were increasingly comprehensive. From here he wrote his two letters to the Corinthians. If you will read them you will see that he canvassed pretty nearly every subject of church organization and of practical sociology: Ought the church to retain in its membership a fornicator? Ought Christians to observe the festivals of the moon? What about eating meats that had been offered to idols? Ought Christians to marry? Ought women to have part in public worship? Ought Christians to have lawsuits? Prompted in part by questions submitted to him, his letters grew to include more and more of doctrinal instruction and of practical application of truth to life. Read these letters and see how there come into them such sublime passages as the chapter on charity (I Cor. 13):

Though I speak with the tongues of men and of angels, and have not charity, I am become as sounding brass or a tinkling cymbal.

And though I have the gift of prophecy, and understand all mysteries, and all knowledge; and though I have all faith, so that I could remove mountains, and have not charity, I am nothing. . . .

Charity suffereth long, and is kind; charity envieth not; charity vaunteth not itself, is not puffed up,

Doth not behave itself unseemly, seeketh not her own, is not easily provoked, thinketh no evil,

Rejoiceth not in iniquity, but rejoiceth in the truth;

Beareth all things, believeth all things, hopeth all things, endureth all things. . . .

And now abideth faith, hope, charity, these three; but the greatest of these is charity.

And his great chapter on life after death (I Cor. 15):

For this corruptible must put on incorruption, and this mortal must put on immortality.

So when this corruptible shall have put on incorruption, and this mortal shall have put on immortality, then shall be brought to pass the saying that is written, Death is swallowed up in victory.

O death, where is thy sting? O grave, where is thy victory? . . .

Therefore, my beloved brethren, be ye steadfast, unmoveable, always abounding in the work of the Lord, forasmuch as ye know that your labour is not in vain in the Lord.

The Epistle to the Hebrews, which in our Bible is attributed to Paul, was almost certainly not written by him. The style is very different from his, and it does not seem likely that he would have addressed a letter particularly to Jews. The best Greek composition in the New Testament is in this letter, and so delicate and persuasive is it that there are those who think they detect a woman's hand. Some have conjectured that Priscilla (Acts 18:1) might have been the writer. In her home Paul had a lodging, and she and Aquila, her husband, were among his very best friends.

The letter is general, but its definite purpose is to convince thoughtful Jews that they will lose nothing by embracing the new faith but, on the contrary, will gain. It says: "You can have all that you cherish most and even more in the Christian faith. Do you love your Law? Well you may, but here is the same law written more beautifully. Do you love your temple, your priesthood, your traditions? Everything you have cared for is here, and all the better."

It is noble in its conception of the basic principle of all heroism—faith. It calls the long roll of the faithful in all the ages and says that widely as they differed in many things they were all animated by one common inspiration. Read this grand roll call in chapter eleven:

They were stoned, they were sawn asunder, were tempted, were slain with the sword: they wandered about in sheepskins and goatskins; being destitute, afflicted, tormented; . . .

. . . they wandered in deserts, and in mountains, and in dens and caves of the earth. . . .

Wherefore seeing we also are compassed about with so great a cloud of witnesses, let us lay aside every weight, and the sin which doth so easily beset us, and let us run with patience the race that is set before us.

Others of the apostles now began to write. James, the brother of Jesus, had never felt wholly satisfied with Paul's doctrine of faith; he wrote a letter, a strange one for a man of such devotion to the law, of which one might almost say that it was not religious at all, so little did it regard form or ceremony. It was a very practical little homily on the importance of good works:

Pure religion and undefiled before God and the Father is this, To visit the fatherless and widows in their affliction, and to keep himself unspotted from the world.

A younger brother of Jesus, named Jude, also wrote a short letter. It was rather an apology for not writing a longer one which he had in mind to write on "our common Christianity." It grew out of a special occasion, which it may be presumed to have met well.

John, the son of Zebedee, also wrote, though later, three letters, one a remarkably sweet and beautiful letter addressed to no one in particular, and two short ones. Of these two, one was to a Christian lady whose name we do not know and the other to a friend, Gaius. Peter, also, wrote two letters and rather fine ones, as might have been expected of this blunt courageous man. But no one employed this method to the extent that Paul did. His letters were copied and lent and read and became a kind of unofficial manual for the administration of the churches.

Paul left Ephesus after the riot, but not to return to Jerusalem; he was going across into Europe again. We may imagine the conversation that took place, for we get a wonderful glimpse into his mind in the letters to the Corinthians.

"You are going over the same ground again, Paul?"

"Yes, but every time widening the circle. This is my third time out, and each time I make a little larger swing, and see the work growing."

"When do you get back to Jerusalem?"

"Next spring at Easter. I am going to take back the biggest collection that the Jerusalem church ever received."

"Are you going to stay there?"

"Stay there? Do you think I could ever be content to settle down and stay in Jerusalem?"

"But you are getting to be an old man, and travel is hard on you and dangerous."

"Yes, I have been in dangers of many kinds. It has been my privilege to travel farther than any of the other apostles,

> in labours more abundant, in stripes above measure, in prisons more frequent, in deaths oft.
> Of the Jews five times received I forty stripes save one.
> Thrice was I beaten with rods, once was I stoned, thrice I suffered shipwreck, a night and a day I have been in the deep;
> In journeyings often, in perils of waters, in perils of robbers, in perils by mine own countrymen, in perils by the heathen, in perils in the city, in perils in the wilderness, in perils in the sea, in perils among false brethren;
> In weariness and painfulness, in watchings often, in hunger and thirst, in fastings often, in cold and nakedness."

"That is a long list of perils, Paul. It must nearly have broken you down."

"I have still a heavier burden, my anxiety for all the churches I have established."

"Do you carry them on your mind and feel responsible for them?"

"Who is weak and I am not weak? Who is caused to stumble and I burn not?"

"You have done a great work and have much to be proud of."

"I am proud of it, and have been criticized as being vain about it. I have sometimes been ashamed of myself for letting people know my pride and joy in all this. Yet, while I have sometimes made myself a fool by seeming to boast, I really am not boastful. God forbid that I should glory, save in the cross of Christ and in the joy of service."

"When you go out again where shall you go?"

"Back again over the same ground, but more widely, to all the Roman sub-capitals in Asia Minor and Greece, and then to Rome."

"Rome? And what then?"

"Oh, then I rather think I shall go to Spain."

Spain was a long way off and was bounded by the Pillars of Hercules, which we now call the Straits of Gibraltar. They were supposed to bear a banner in the sky above them, saying, "Ne plus ultra," nothing more beyond. Paul was going the limit.

He set forth on his journey, and it was while he was on the road, at Cenchrea, that an incident happened which gave us the greatest of all his epistles. A woman named Phebe, "who had been a helper of many and of Paul also," was going to Rome and asked Paul for a letter of introduction, which, he, never having been to Rome, agreed to write. Phebe suggested that it would be well for Paul to tell the Roman Christians some of his teachings, as she was afraid she might not be able to answer their questions. He agreed to do it if she could find him a stenographer, and Phebe produced a young man named Tertius. He proved a good helper, and so Paul expanded his teachings into a more fully developed system than anywhere else in his writings. He was not sidetracked by questions concerning local matters and he swung out free into his orbit. Phebe took the letter with her and delivered it safely to the Romans. It is a great achievement and was written just before Paul, with his committee of provincial Christians and his goodly collection for the mother church, went up to Jerusalem for what proved to be his last visit.

He had been warned. A certain prophet, Agabus, who had come down from Judea, met him at Cæsarea, took Paul's girdle and bound his hands and feet, saying:

Thus saith the Holy Ghost, So shall the Jews at Jerusalem bind the man that owneth this girdle, and shall deliver him into the hands of the Gentiles.

And when we heard these things [says Doctor Luke] both we, and they of that place, besought him not to go up to Jerusalem.

Then Paul answered, What mean ye to weep and to break mine heart? for I am ready not to be bound only, but also to die at Jerusalem for the name of the Lord Jesus.

So, seeing that they could not dissuade him, they went with him. He took the large collection, as he had expected, and was well received by the apostles, though still looked at a little askance because of his free doctrines. Only a few days had passed, however, when he was seized by the local authorities as "the man that teacheth all men everywhere against the people, and the law," and was thrown into jail. There, weary of delays in the local courts, he finally exercised his right as a Roman citizen and appealed to Cæsar, who at that time was Nero. Thus it was that Paul came to Rome.

Doctor Luke stayed with him through the two years of imprisonment which preceded his appeal, journeyed with him in a winter voyage and shipwreck, and a sojourn of three months in Malta, all of which he describes vividly in The Acts. They reached Rome together, and there the book of The Acts ends abruptly:

And Paul dwelt two whole years in his own

hired house, and received all that came in unto
him,

Preaching the kingdom of God, and teaching
those things which concern the Lord Jesus Christ,
with all confidence, no man forbidding him.

Probably no one came up from Jerusalem to
Rome to appear against him, for five years had
elapsed since his arrest, and so he was acquitted
at his first trial and allowed to live under sur-
veillance but in comfort. During those years
he wrote more letters, including some of the
finest, like Ephesians and Colossians, and especially Philippians. He had a special love for
the places where he was whipped and imprisoned
and where he compelled the magistrates to come
down to the jail and invite him to walk out. It
was in this period, also, that he wrote the charm-
ing little personal letter to Philemon.

It happened in this way. Philemon was a
Christian man of wealth who lived in Asia
Minor. He had a slave named Onesimus, a wild
and disobedient lad who ran away and got to
Rome, where he led a gay life. But he knew
Paul, who had been at his master's house, and
he went to hear him preach. Homesick and con-
science-smitten, he asked what he ought to do.
Paul kept him a while to test him and then
suggested that he go back to his master, not

under bonds but of his own free will, and Paul wrote a letter requesting his old friend to take this lad back on a new basis, "as a brother in the Lord." Paul was in a good and almost merry mood when he wrote this letter: "I will get around in your neighborhood after a while. Have a room ready for me."

It was not at all a depressed and broken down apostle who was writing, you see. In some ways he was having a very good time. He was not in prison but was living under guard in "his own hired house," a splendid host, entertaining pilgrims from far and near. Where did he get the money? We can only guess. In some way apparently he had come into funds. Perhaps his father had died and left him an inheritance. Perhaps his well-to-do friends kept his purse filled. It must have cost him thirty thousand dollars, as an eminent scholar once computed, for those five years, six thousand dollars a year for rent in Rome, where rents were high and the housing problem was acute, and for food for his rather large household, and for his expense of transportation for himself and his companions. Thirty thousand dollars for a man who had boasted that he was poor yet made many rich, and that his own hands had supported him much of the time while preaching!

Wherever the money came from it is a fine thing for us all that during those five years Paul had it. Never, probably, has the world better spent thirty thousand dollars. He had a guard, whom, of course, he had to feed and fee, and this guard had to listen to Paul, who was always talking to visitors and telling about Jesus. The soldier who guarded him to-day might be on guard at the palace the next day, or at least might sleep that night with palace guards. It was not long till Paul could write:

> But I would ye should understand, brethren, that the things which happened unto me have fallen out rather unto the furtherance of the gospel:
> So that my bonds in Christ are manifest in all the palace, and in all other places;
> And many of the brethren in the Lord, waxing confident by my bonds, are much more bold to speak the word without fear.

Before many months there were disciples under the very roof of Nero, and Paul could add:

> All the saints salute you, chiefly they that are of Cæsar's household.

After about two years, as we suppose, the case against him was dismissed for lack of prosecution, and he made another journey of which we get scattered glimpses in his two espistles to Timothy and the one to Titus. He had been in Crete and other islands and again at Troas. There is a verse which seems inconsequential, but it is luminous; it comes in the sad but triumphant ending of his last letter to Timothy, pleading with him to come to Rome and help care for him, and to bring Mark. Paul had learned that Mark was a better man than he had thought him.

> Only Luke is with me. Take Mark, and bring him with thee: for he is profitable to me for the ministry. . . .
> The cloak that I left at Troas with Carpus, when thou comest, bring with thee, and the books, but especially the parchments.

When had Paul been at Troas? The only occasion on which we saw him there was in 51, and this was 58! Was he asking for a cloak that he had left seven years before? No, he must have been out of prison and making another great swing around his circle, when he was arrested a second time.

His second imprisonment was very different. No longer was he in his own house but, if we may trust tradition, was in the Mamertine prison of which Hawthorne wrote, "Methinks there cannot be on earth another so evil a den, so full of haunting memories and vague surmises." The difference was that the first offense was only against the Jews, while now Christianity had grown so fast that the Roman government had begun to fear. How long his second imprisonment lasted we do not know, but there came the dark day when they led him out and killed him. Peter, if we are to believe tradition, had also come to Rome and when sentenced to die asked to be crucified head downward, deeming himself unworthy to be killed in the same manner as his Lord—a magnificent touch of sentiment in a rough old saint.

It is almost certain that Nero blotted out both these great lives. We have an epistle of Peter's written from "Babylon," by which we suppose he meant Rome, and at the time of writing it he seems not to have been in any immediate danger. But the test came, and he met it gloriously. As for Paul, he died triumphant.

> For I am now ready to be offered, and the time of my departure is at hand.
> I have fought a good fight, I have finished my course, I have kept the faith;
> Henceforth there is laid up for me a crown of righteousness.

And nobly had he won it. But to the end he wanted books, and white paper; and he besought his young friend Timothy not to forget them.

More knowledge to gain, more epistles to write! His conquering soul went marching on.

So we end our glance at the Epistles. There remains the last book in the Bible, the book of Revelation. It is a much abused book. The first thing necessary is to forget most that you have heard about it. It is not a program of coming events. It has in it nothing about the next presidential election in the United States, nor anything about the Pope or the Kaiser. Its chief character is Nero. Indeed, the book is so simple it is hard to make readers believe its true explanation.

Remember, first, that in the interval between the Old and the New Testaments apocalyptic literature became enormously popular. There was a flood of books with dragons and grotesque animals representing peoples or nations or events. The Jewish imagination reveled in this style, which is illustrated in a part of Daniel, a very late book of the Maccabæan period, and much more dramatically in Revelation. At one time it seemed that all other literature in the Christian church might be drowned out by the flood of this florid material.

Just after Paul and Peter were killed, John, the apostle, was banished to the island of Patmos. He was not yet the aged apostle of love; he was a hot-headed "son of thunder" and he wanted to write letters of encouragement to the churches in Asia Minor, the principal ones being seven in number. The letters, molded on a common form but straightforward enough, are in the opening chapters of Revelation. But John wanted to say something else and to say it in a way that would not get the people who had the letter in their possession into trouble. So he adopted the popular cryptic form which makes up the balance of the book. It should be studied through an opera-glass and not a microscope. There is no use asking what is the meaning of every hair on the tail of each fantastic beast; the colors are put on with a big brush. But the three ideas are plain as a pike staff. Those ideas are:

First: Do not be afraid of the persecutions that originate in Jerusalem. That city will soon be in trouble with Rome and not able to persecute Christians.

Second: Do not be afraid of the emperor of the mighty city on the seven hills that now is ruling the world; that city has trouble of its own coming, and it is not far off.

Third: Hold to your faith, for it will survive. Jesus Christ is greater than Nero, and His religion will last longer than the Roman government.

The author spelled out Nero's name in a cryptogram, making the number 666. He disguised thinly the main things that he had to say. A Roman official who picked it up would have thrown it aside, saying, "What's this wearisome stuff? I haven't time to bother with it." Whereas if John had put his meaning into plain Greek any man having it in his possession would have been beheaded, and too many good men were losing their heads as it was.

How amazingly his great dream came true! The Roman Empire fell, and the one power that could avail to save it, not from the pagans but to the future through the pagans, was not the political or judicial power of Rome or the culture of Athens. That which saved civilization when Jerusalem was destroyed and Rome sacked by the vandals was nothing more or less than the Church of Christ. Read Gibbon's *Decline and Fall of the Roman Empire* and you get, from a rather unsympathetic scholar of cold temperament, the narrative of how it all came about. Even he warms and kindles as he tells about it.

But first read The Acts, the Epistles, and even fanciful, cryptic, vehement Revelation.

V

TEN GREAT MEN OF THE BIBLE

QUESTIONS

1. What general reduced his army in order to win a victory?
   Judges 7.

2. What great leader lost his strength and leadership because a woman cut off his hair?
   Judges 16:18-20.

3. Who trapped and killed a lion in the snow?
   II Samuel 23:20.

4. What general, though thirsty, refused to drink water which his men had risked their lives to bring him?
   II Samuel 23:13-17.

5. What prophet was admonished by words of wisdom from an ass?
   Numbers 22:30.

6. What king divided his kingdom by refusing to modify the policy of his wise father?
   I Kings 12:68.

7. When did one apostle rebuke another?
   Galatians 2:11.

8. What child did Whittier have in mind when he wrote a poem in condemnation of Daniel Webster?
   I Samuel 4:21.

9. What woman established a place of worship with money that her son had stolen and refunded?
   Judges 17.

10. When did seers begin to be called prophets?
    I Samuel 9:9.

11. Who sent his servant to select a wife for his son?
    Genesis 24:2.
12. What man was counted inspired of God to be a
    good worker in metals?
    Exodus 35:30-35.
13. Who was the successor of Judas?
    Acts 1:24-26.
14. Who saw a vision of animals let down from the
    sky on a large canvas?
    Acts 10:9-16.
15. What New Testament book is the letter of an
    apostle to a woman?
    John 2.

V

TEN GREAT MEN OF THE BIBLE

TEN thousand ministers of all religious denominations were asked to name the ten greatest men in the Bible. It was not intended to include the name of Jesus Christ, but still His name led many lists and would, of course, have stood first in all. We have devoted to His life the whole of one chapter, and this one is to treat of ten others.

The second name in order of the number of votes is that of St. Paul; the next is Moses, and the third, David. These are in practically all the lists. After these three the vote is more evenly distributed. The total number of men named is sixty, and some of those that have the smallest number of votes are accompanied by the best reasons for inclusion. From this notable list, probably the most interesting poll ever made on Bible characters, we select the following names, not in the order of their plurality but in chronological arrangement:

1. Adam, the first man with conscience and a knowledge of moral responsibility.

2.   Noah, the man on whom at one time hung the hope of civilization.

3.   Abraham, the prince of pioneers.

4.   Joseph, political economist; man of vision and integrity.

5.   Moses, lawgiver, creator of a nation, founder of the world's system of legislation.

6.   David, shepherd, soldier, singer and king.

7.   Jeremiah, most heroic of that heroic group, the prophets.

8.   Judas Maccabæus, the rebuilder of a nation.

9.   John the Baptist, the herald of the dawn.

10.   Saint Paul, apostle, traveler, author and martyr.

The reason for the larger number of names in the Old Testament is doubtless to be explained by the longer period which it covers. The New Testament narrative, from the beginning of the ministry of Jesus until the destruction of Jerusalem by Titus, is only about forty years, whereas the Old Testament traverses many centuries.

1.   ADAM

Whether you get your story of creation from Genesis or from Mr. Wells, the broad outlines are the same—a formless mass of matter in motion, evolving gradually into land and water, producing vegetation, and the lowest forms of life. Then higher forms, and still higher, until finally there came one amazing individual who raised himself upon his lower limbs and dared to say, "I am different from the rest."

At first he had a hard time defining the difference. He ate and drank like other animals. He reproduced his species in the same gross sensual way. The lusts of appetite ran in his veins with as hot a tide as in the beasts about him. He killed other animals and ate their raw and quivering flesh. Yet he was not like them. He walked unsteadily in an erect posture, and that was a distinction of no small significance, for it left the upper limbs free to serve the head while the lower limbs, less fleet than those of the horse or ass, were yet strong and capable of rapid motion.

He had a brain over-arched by a skull of noble curvature, a tiny reproduction of the blue curve of the sky. It was this brain within this marvelous arch that pulled him up and gave him a sphere of vision unique in creation. The eagle could see farther in its flight; the ape had a wider radius when he climbed, but he, the man, and he alone, could look forward and outward and up.

With some such vague but awe-inspiring

strokes history sketches for us the portrait of our first ancestor and leaves him naked, unhonored, nameless. Genesis is much more definite. It gives us his name, Adam, and his dwelling place, "a garden eastward in Eden."

> And out of the ground made the Lord God to grow every tree that is pleasant to the sight, and good for food; the tree of life also in the midst of the garden, and the tree of knowledge of good and evil.

We witness the creation of the first woman:

> And the Lord caused a deep sleep to fall upon Adam, and he slept: and he took one of his ribs, and closed up the flesh instead thereof;
> And the rib, which the Lord God had taken from man, made he a woman, and brought her unto the man.
> And Adam said, This is now bone of my bones, and flesh of my flesh: she shall be called Woman because she was taken out of Man.
> Therefore shall a man leave his father and his mother, and shall cleave unto his wife: and they shall be one flesh.

Of all the trees in the garden they might eat the fruit, except one only, the tree of the knowledge of good and evil. But lured on by the serpent, they did eat of the fruit of that. They were discovered and promptly punished. The tribe of the serpent bears forever the signs of his punishment:

> And the Lord God said unto the serpent, Because thou hast done this, thou art cursed above all cattle, and above every beast of the field; upon thy belly shalt thou go, and dust shalt thou eat all the days of thy life.

As for Adam and Eve, they were cast out of the garden. The ground was cursed with weeds and thistles; hard work and the sweat of their brows was to be their portion until they should return to the dust from which they came. So the Lord

> drove out the man; and he placed at the east of the garden of Eden Cherubims, and a flaming sword which turned every way, to keep the way of the tree of life.

A million sermons have been preached about Adam, berating him for his lost innocence, bemoaning his fall. How many of those sermons have overlooked the most significant phase of the story! Adam was innocent in the Garden, in the same sense that the sheep were innocent, and the sheep are just as innocent now as they were then. But Adam in Eden had no *character,* and character is the one good thing which God alone does not create. It is a joint product.

Just what the sin was which is recorded under the symbol of the tree and its fruit we do not know. It is an admirable symbol. The birds in Eden pecked holes in the fruit of that tree, as of many others. No fruit-eating beasts held it in special regard. Adam's sin was something which was wrong for him but not wrong for beasts and birds, some act of unbridled lust or bloody revenge; and having done it, he knew instantly that it was wrong. Somehow, in this new green universe, remorse and repentance entered into the soul of a living creature; and character began.

"A being such as I should be capable of something better," he said to himself.

Why did he say it?

What made him say it?

How was it that he knew himself to be different from the beasts that perish? Why was he so sure that it was wrong for him and not for them to use his brief opportunity for all it was worth? What persuaded him that God cared?

No matter if the story in Genesis be an allegory; no matter if it summarize in the experience of one man a process which worked itself out through generations or centuries. The central fact remains, that one day *somebody* stood out against a background of innocent and contented animalism and assumed the self-consciousness and reproach which go with a moral nature. To that somebody, that Adam, we owe a debt which we can never repay. He was earth's first great hero.

Adam in the Garden, fattening on the fruits that grew without labor, has had too much attention. We care little for that brief inglorious period in his existence. It could not last long. Let us rather remember the later Adam, contending with thorns and thistles, trying hard to govern the rising generation which perplexed him as it has perplexed succeeding fathers, the Adam who earned his bread with the sweat of his brow, the Adam whose eldest son killed his younger brother, the Adam who courageously, uncomplainingly carried on and handed down to his descendants a nature capable of responding to law and duty. That Adam is the first in honor as well as in time. He and Eve sent down to us the qualities that lift us out of the dust from which they came and back to which we, like them, return.

2. NOAH

Times of comfort and peace have brief histories. It is only when changes threaten and disaster impends that History dips her pen and adjusts her far-sighted spectacles to discover the nobleman.

And God saw that the wickedness of man was great in the earth, and that every imagination of the thoughts of the heart was only evil continually. . . .

And the Lord said, I will destroy man whom I have created from the face of the earth.

Carlyle said that no age need go down to destruction if only there arise a man who knows his times and can lead. Noah had one of these qualifications but not the other. He could not lead. He preached for one hundred and twenty years to an ever-diminishing congregation. At the last he had only his own family standing by him, and was lucky to be able to hold even them.

You can imagine the derisive comments of his neighbors. Forty days and nights of rain, indeed! It never had happened before, it never could happen. Noah was a crazy old fool. Thus they commented, misplacing his tools no doubt and laughing as he hunted for them; thinking up new ways to annoy him and new practical jokes to perpetrate. "How's the weather this morning, old fellow? Doesn't look much like rain to me. When's your flood coming anyway? Guess maybe it ain't never coming."

But it did come!

In the six hundredth year of Noah's life, in the second month, the seventeenth day of the month, the same day were all the fountains of the great deep broken up, and the windows of heaven were opened.

And the rain was upon the earth forty days and forty nights. . . .

And every living substance was destroyed.

It is an interesting question for every man to ask himself: "If I had been on the earth in the days of Noah, should I have been one of the survivors or one of the wise ones who knew it all? If *I* had been in Jerusalem in the days of Jesus, should I have been one of the few who saw Truth, even in its rough peasant garb, or should I have stood with the respectable, well fed majority, shouting, 'Away with this disturber. Crucify'? If *I* had been in the colonies in the days of George Washington, am I quite sure that I should have risked my property and future with an ill-fed, ill-conditioned army of rebels? Shouldn't I perhaps have considered the Tories a much more substantial, sane and respectable lot?"

Only a few have courage and vision to stand against the crowd; Noah had both in plentiful amounts.

Thus did Noah; according to all that God commanded him, so did he.

A grand tribute to a man who stood firm and true when humanity as a whole went wrong. He did what God told him to do, and he was justified in the result.

And then?

If you or I had written the story we should have pictured the serene old age of Noah, in his uniform as a retired admiral of the navy, introduced to the fast multiplying posterity of mankind as the man who saved the world. We should have provided for him a future worthy of his great achievement. The record shocks us:

> And Noah was drunken.

Drunk perhaps with his success. Drunk with pride when people told him how all his weather predictions had come true. Drunk with the praise which he had richly earned and could not wisely appreciate. Drunk also with wine.

A shameful scene as he lay in his tent, Ham peering in with mocking laughter, and the other sons doing their sorrowful duty—a scene worthy of the reproach which Whittier wrote of Daniel Webster after his Seventh of March speech:

> So fallen—So lost! The light withdrawn
>   Which once he wore!
> The glory of his gray hairs gone
>   Forevermore! . . .

Then pay the reverence of old days
    To his dead fame;
Walk backward with averted gaze
    And hide his shame!

Noah was drunken. The man who had saved
the world did not continue in the work of its
salvation. The new age that followed the flood
had to find new leaders for its new problems.
Yet so long as the rainbow overarches the storm
cloud the world shall remember the integrity
and courage and obedience of Noah.

And God remembered Noah.

Let us not forget him.

3. ABRAHAM

Most of the pioneers since the world began
have lived and died and left no memory of their
deeds. They blazed the trails which those who
followed trod to paths, and by the time that
these had become macadamized highways it was
too late to find the record of him whose adventurous feet had first passed that way. Edward
Everett Hale found himself profoundly moved
by his contemplation of the nameless saints
whose heroism we have inherited:

190

TEN GREAT MEN OF THE BIBLE

What was his name? I do not know his name;
I only know he heard God's voice and came,
Brought all he loved across the sea,
And came to work for God and me;
Felled the ungracious oak,
Dragged from the soil
With horrid toil
The thrice-gnarled root and stubborn rock,
With plenty piled the mountain side,
And then, at length, without memorial died.
No pealing trumpet thunders forth his fame;
He lived, he died: I do not know his name.

But a few of the heroic adventurers left authentic records that defy the effects of oblivion. Prince of the pioneers is Abraham. He lived, as his ancestors had lived, in the fertile valley of Mesopotamia, a great landowner and shepherd.

And Abram was very rich in cattle, in silver, and in gold.

Lot, his son-in-law, was also rich.

And the land was not able to bear them, that they might dwell together: . . .
And there was strife between the herdmen of Abram's cattle and the herdmen of Lot's cattle.

More pasture was needed for their flocks, and to their neighbors that was a sufficient explanation of their migration; just as many historians regard "economic pressure" as the whole explanation of the journey of the Pilgrim Fathers and of so many other important movements in history. But there is something in men which responds to an impulse other than the mere need for more food, or the desire for wealth.

> Now the Lord said unto Abram, Get thee out of thy country, and from thy kindred, and from thy father's house, unto a land that I will shew thee.
> And he went out, not knowing whither he went.

In those two sentences, one from the Old Testament, the other from the New, you have the real story of Abraham's migration. He was already on the way when the message came to him. It is interesting that his father, Terah, had heard a similar message years before and had started but never arrived.

> And Terah took Abram his son . . . and they went forth from Ur of the Chaldees, to go into the land of Canaan; and they came unto Haran and dwelt there.

Ur of the Chaldees was a city where the worship of the moon was the supreme form of religion. Terah revolted against it and, hearing the voice of the Lord, started to get away from the land of idolatry. But he got only as far as

Haran, and, though the worship of the moon was in full swing there also, he settled down. With the growing tolerance of age, the moon worship did not seem so bad as it had in the fresh idealism of youth.

> Terah, the father of Abraham, . . . served other gods.

He was old and tired. Nothing appeared quite so important as it had. Why raise a fuss with the neighbors? Better accept things as they are and rest easy. So Terah compromised. But his life was not a total failure. At least he had started, and, while he did not arrive, he made the journey easier for Abraham. Of how many other lives was his life typical—men who aspire to be pioneers and set out in youth to make the full journey but travel no farther than from Ur to Haran and end by worshipping the same old moon god. Fortunate are they when their sons carry on.

God changed the name of Abram to Abraham.

> Neither shall thy name any more be called Abram, but thy name shall be Abraham; for a father of many nations have I made thee.

He was given children when more than ninety years old, and he lived to be a hundred and seventy-five, "an old man and full of years."

Among many elements which combined to make him great, one is particularly worthy of remembrance—he was the real head of his own household. God said:

> Abraham shall surely become a great and mighty nation, and all the nations of the earth shall be blessed in him.

Why?

> For I know him, that he will *command his children and his household after him*, and they shall keep the way of the Lord, to do justice and judgment.

If leaders were chosen in our day on the basis of their proved power to govern their own families in righteousness, how many would qualify? Maybe that lack in modern men is one reason why there are not more Abrahams.

4. JOSEPH

And Joseph was brought down to Egypt; and Potiphar, an officer of Pharaoh, captain of the guard, bought him of the hands of the Ishmaelites, . . .

And Joseph found grace in his sight, and he served him; and he [Potiphar] made him overseer over his house, and all that he had. . . .

> And it came to pass after these things, that his master's wife cast her eyes upon Joseph; and she said, Lie with me. . . . and he fled, and got him out. . . .

The illicit love of Potiphar's wife, and her revenge when the young overseer refused to betray the trust of his master, is the most widely remembered episode in Joseph's career. It has been the theme of plays and novels, and the cynical writers of all ages have scoffed at the young man's scruples and by their scoffing condemned themselves. For the story of Joseph is the finest single story in the Old Testament.

His father's favorite, and therefore the scorn and envy of his brothers, he made trouble for himself by the strange wisdom of his dreams and by his "coat of many colors," his father's gift. "Behold this dreamer cometh," they sneered, and forthwith they cast him into a pit, and smearing his coat with the blood of a kid took it home to their sorrowing father with a lie.

A commonplace age is always suspicious of dreamers. But what continent was ever opened, what railway built, what great discovery made, without their help?

> He whom a dream hath possessed treads the
> invincible marches;
> From the dust of the day's long road he leaps to
> a laughing star;

And the ruin of worlds that fall he views from
   celestial arches,
And rides God's battlefield in a golden and shining
   car.

The dreamer may ride in the golden car at the
end, as the poets inform us, but he treads a long
hard path in the beginning. The Ishmaelites
bought Joseph when his brothers removed him
from the pit into which they had cast him, and
he tramped beside their camels down the dusty
trail into Egypt. By sheer brains and force of
character he won his way into Potiphar's employ:

And he [Potiphar] left all that he had in
Joseph's hand; and he knew not aught he had, save
the bread which he did eat.

Joseph's life stretched out before him with the
fine promise of success when the passion of a
woman intervened, and evil days descended.
"Behold this dreamer cometh"; unlock the prison
door and let it clang behind him.

In prison who remembered him? Potiphar's
wife, perhaps, with a sinister smile at his
scruples. His guilty brothers, like enough, with
a lessening prick of conscience until they almost
persuaded themselves they had forgotten. But
the people whom he had benefited did not remember him. The chief butler promised not to
forget, but being released "forgat him."

Only God did not forget him, and his dreams, which had been the original cause of his trouble, were finally to bring him release and success. In a previous chapter we have recalled the famous dream of Pharaoh and how, by its interpretation, Joseph was able to organize the food supplies of Egypt so that the abundant harvests of seven years were stored away against the famine of the succeeding seven years. All óther lands were desolate, including the land where his father and guilty brothers dwelt, and at length the brothers are forced to go to Egypt to buy corn; they open negotiations with Egypt's great official.

> And Joseph knew his brethren, but they knew him not.

His hour of revenge had come. For several days he kept them guessing. He locked them up and after their release kept Simeon as a hostage until they should return and bring their little brother Benjamin with them. They promised, and started off. Imagine their surprise when they opened their sacks to find not merely the corn they had come to purchase but the money which they had given in payment. They hurried on to Jacob, their father, and told him how the governor had received them and of his demand that they should bring little Ben-

jamin when they came again. How they went
again to Joseph, still without recognizing him;
how they were received and entertained at his
palace; the trick he played upon them to test
their love for little Benjamin and so stir up the
memory of their different treatment of the other
little brother whom they supposed they had
killed—all this is set forth in a style as fascinat-
ing as any novel.

> And they went up out of Egypt, and came into
> the land of Canaan unto Jacob their father,
> And told him, saying, Joseph is yet alive, and
> he is governor over all the land of Egypt.
> And Jacob's heart fainted, for he believed them
> not.
> And they told him all the words of Joseph which
> he had said unto them: and when he saw the
> wagons which Joseph had sent to carry him, the
> spirit of Jacob their father revived:
> And Israel said, It is enough; Joseph my son is
> yet alive; I will go and see him before I die.

So came the people of Israel into Egypt,
saved by Joseph, whose name was potent enough
to secure protection and provender for them,
not only during his lifetime but for four centuries after his death.

> And the children of Israel were fruitful, and in-
> creased abundantly, and multiplied, and waxed
> mighty; and the land was filled with them.

> Now there arose up a new king over Egypt, which knew not Joseph.

A new king, a new crisis, a new hero to meet the crisis; the next great character of the Old Testament, Moses. It was his part to take the children of Israel out of Egypt, as it had been the work of Joseph to save their lives by getting them in. And when the day of deliverance arrived, and they marched forth into freedom and the wilderness, the procession was led by two strange and holy objects, the ark of God and the bones of Joseph.

> And Moses took the bones of Joseph with him: for he had straitly sworn the children of Israel, saying, God will surely visit you [he was a dreamer, you see, to the end]; and ye shall carry up my bones away hence with you.

5. MOSES

A celebrated clergyman, in recounting the curious happenings of a long ministry, said that the strangest letter he ever received was as follows:

> Reverend Sir: I will be at your church next Sunday morning and will deposit one dollar in the collection box if you will preach a sermon on the following text: "Put forth thine hand, and take it by the tail."

Just why the letter-writer should have picked out that particular verse, or why the story should have stayed in my mind, I do not know. But I looked up the passage and from time to time I have amused myself by asking other clergymen if they knew where it occurs. The usual guess is that it has to do with the story of Balaam's ass or with Saint Paul, who was attacked by a serpent while gathering wood for a fire after his shipwreck. As a matter of fact, it is to be found in the early part of the record of Moses.

Reared as the grandson of an emperor, doted on by a royal foster mother, Moses, who might have had every luxury, preferred, like Abraham, like each of the prophets, like John the Baptist and Saint Paul, to be "not disobedient to the Heavenly vision." He was modest, as most men of genius are.

> And Moses said unto God, Who am I, that I should go unto Pharaoh, and bring forth the children of Israel out of Egypt? . . .
> Behold, they will not believe me, nor hearken unto my voice: for they will say, The Lord hath not appeared unto thee.
> And the Lord said unto him, What is in thine hand? And he said, a rod.
> And he said, Cast it on the ground. And he cast it on the ground, and it became a serpent; and Moses fled from before it.

And the Lord said unto Moses, Put forth thine
hand, and take it by the tail. And he put forth
his hand, and caught it, and it became a rod in
his hand.

That rod was to play a mighty part in the
history of the next forty years. By it the
plagues were brought upon the Egyptians in
tragic succession until even the stubborn will of
Pharaoh was broken; the Red Sea divided at its
touch to let the children of Israel pass through;
and in the wilderness, when water failed, the
rock which it smote gave forth a crystal stream.
Moses had need of its help and of all the encouragement and support that Aaron, his
colleague, and the strong men of the twelve
tribes could give, for these undisciplined ex-
slaves whom he led into the wilderness were
impatient, restless and addicted to grumbling at
every opportunity. As law-giver, military com-
mander and executive, he transformed them into
a self-governing people, and left a body of laws
which have come down to our own day as the
foundation of modern jurisprudence and civic
sanitation.

There have been many leaders of powerful
personality who failed because they could not
associate strong men with them. Moses was not
one of these. He realized clearly the necessity

for first-class helpers. He needed the wise counsel of Jethro, who saw clearly that the combined
duties of administrator and judge were too much
for any one man and urged Moses to set up a
group of associate judges.

> And Moses' father in law said unto him, The
> thing that thou doest is not good.
> Thou wilt surely wear away, both thou, and this
> people that is with thee: for this thing is too heavy
> for thee; thou art not able to perform it thyself
> alone.

He needed the sword of Joshua. He needed
the eloquence and priestly help of Aaron.

> And Moses said unto the Lord, O my Lord, I
> am not eloquent . . . but I am slow of speech,
> and of a slow tongue. . . .
> And the anger of the Lord was kindled against
> Moses, and he said, Is not Aaron the Levite thy
> brother? I know that he can speak well. . . .
> And thou shalt speak unto him, and put words
> in his mouth: . . .
> And he shall be to thee instead of a mouth, and
> thou shalt be to him instead of God.

The special talent of each of these associates
supplemented his own abilities, and he was big
enough to know that they required supplement-
ing. But the great essentials—courage, idealism,
vision, faith—he borrowed from no man. He
had them in abundance.

For forty years he carried the burden. One by one his contemporaries dropped away, leaving him an old man among a nation of children. We catch a glimpse of the towering lonely spirit in the one Psalm which long and venerable tradition declares to have come from him, the ninetieth:

> Lord, thou hast been our dwelling place in all generations.
>
> Before the mountains were brought forth, or ever thou hadst formed the earth and the world, even from everlasting to everlasting, thou art God. . . .
>
> For a thousand years in thy sight are but as yesterday when it is past, and as a watch in the night.
>
> Thou carriest them away as with a flood; they are as a sleep: in the morning they are like grass which groweth up.
>
> In the morning it flourisheth and groweth up; in the evening it is cut down, and withereth. . . .
>
> So teach us to number our days, that we may apply our hearts unto wisdom.

"The days of our years are threescore years and ten;" said the same Psalm, "and if by reason of strength they be fourscore years, yet is their strength labour and sorrow." His own years, however, were many more.

> And Moses was an hundred and twenty years
> old when he died; his eye was not dim, nor his
> natural force abated.

He died without ever setting foot upon the
Promised Land, toward which he had kept his
people pointed through the weary years. Like
so many other men of vision he never quite
realized his whole ideal. But his was the leadership in the formative years of the nation; his the
joy of standing side by side upon the mountain
with God and there receiving the moral law
that was to make all the difference between his
followers and the heathen whom they were to
meet and overcome. His was the vision from
Mount Nebo of the fertile land which his people
would inherit but in which he himself would
never dwell. The checkered centuries have not
obliterated the high significance of his work
nor carried his people back into Egyptian bond-
age.

> And there arose not a prophet since in Israel
> like unto Moses, whom the Lord knew face to face.

6. DAVID

As long as the nature of boys remains what it
always has been David will have a fresh army of
admirers with each new generation, for he is the

original of all Jack-the-giant-killer stories and has been the hero of boyhood for three thousand years.

With the exception of St. Paul no human character occupies so large a place in the Bible; of none are we given so vivid and compelling a picture. The most minute traits and characteristics are set forth in such a way as to make certain that the portrait was drawn from life. What a portrait and what a life! A red-headed shepherd boy, tending his flocks and playing his tunes in the lonesome fields, he is sent up to the army at the critical moment when its forces are paralyzed by the menace of the giant Goliath. What the swords of the stoutest warriors have been powerless to accomplish, he achieves by a well directed shot from his shepherd's sling and becomes immediately a national idol. Triumphantly he is carried to the court while the bands play and the pretty girls sing and dance.

> And the women answered one another as they played, and said, Saul hath slain his thousands, and David his ten thousands.

Small wonder that Michal, the king's daughter, loved him and became his wife; small wonder that Jonathan, the king's son, formed a friendship with him which is one of the most beautiful in all history. Small wonder either that the king himself was jealous and resentful.

> And Saul was very wroth, and the saying displeased him; and he said, They have ascribed unto David ten thousands, and to me they have ascribed but thousands: and what can he have more but the kingdom?
> And Saul eyed David from that day and forward.

The jealous eyes of Saul, who was in a place too big for him and finally went mad trying to fill it, drove David out of the court and into the wilderness where soldiers of fortune rallied to him from various motives, and built up a lusty young army which, to his credit, he kept well disciplined and free from the grosser crimes of guerrilla warfare. Neither the king's forces nor his plots could prevail against the young man's destiny. Fate had picked him out for rulership, and Samuel the prophet had placed the seal of approval upon his claims; he was made for the throne and to it in due course he came.

In a previous chapter we have referred to his conquests, his qualities as an administrator, the sin which forms the one black spot upon his reputation, a sin, by the way, which was not so extraordinary in a king of that period and would perhaps have been forgotten but for the magnificent humility of his repentance, and the Psalms that are his eternal claim to remembrance. We know that his administration was notable for justice:

> And David reigned over all Israel; and David executed judgment and justice unto all his people.

We are told that he was always accessible:

> And when the woman of Tekoah spake to the king, she fell on her face to the ground, and did obeisance, and said, Help, O king.
> And the king said unto her, What aileth thee? And she answered, I am indeed a widow woman, and mine husband is dead.

We know that he solidified his kingdom and made it respected among the powerful nations of that part of the world.

Let us pass by, then, the record of his official life and touch on two incidents that reveal his heart. It was after one of the great battles with the Philistines when his little force was surrounded, cut off from supplies and even from water, that David, worn out and thirsty, thought of the clear pure water in his father's well which had cooled his lips in boyhood. His parched throat yearned for it.

And David longed, and said, Oh that one would give me drink of the water of the well of Bethlehem, which is by the gate!

And the three mighty men brake through the host of the Philistines, and drew water out of the well of Bethlehem, that was by the gate, and took it, and brought it to David: nevertheless he would not drink thereof, but poured it out unto the Lord.

And he said, Be it far from me, O Lord, that I should do this: is not this the blood of the men that went in jeopardy of their lives? therefore he would not drink it.

It is easy to understand why men worshipped a leader like that.

The other incident occurred in the campaign against his son Absalom, the boy whom he loved more than all the world and who repaid his love by organizing a revolt and attempting to seize the throne. David gave orders that the boy was under no circumstances to be killed, but the zeal of a professional soldier was not to be curbed by such an order, and word was brought to the king that Absalom was dead. The revolt was broken, his throne was safe, he could go back to the security of the palace, but it all meant nothing. The feelings of the monarch were swallowed up in the heart-breaking anguish of the father.

O my son Absalom, my son, my son Absalom!

would God I had died for thee, O Absalom, my son, my son!

Perhaps the most poignant cry in history from a father's bleeding heart.

The faults of David are set forth none the less clearly than his virtues; we feel the reality of him in every line. Yet no catalogue of his shortcomings can hide his essential greatness. He was a genius in war, in administration and in literature. He reorganized a government that lasted more than four centuries as a single dynasty and which lived as an ideal through thirty centuries. His songs hurled Cromwell's men singing into the thick of the fight:

> Far below the Roundheads rode,
> And hummed their surly hymn.

It was David's hymn which they sang:

> Let God arise; let his enemies be scattered: let them also that hate him flee before him.

And the same songs have sent the centuries forward marching to the music of hope:

> The Lord is my light and my salvation; whom shall I fear? The Lord is the strength of my life; of whom shall I be afraid?

7. JEREMIAH

It is a terrible handicap to the memory of a man when a descriptive phrase or adjective attaches to his name, for people feel that they are thereby relieved from learning anything more about him. Thus "the patience of Job" has effectually cloaked the real significance of that heroic figure; "as meek as Moses" has distorted the grandeur of one of the really great leaders of history, and the adjective "doubting Thomas" has libeled the brave soul who cried, "Let us also go up with Him that we may die with Him." Similarly, Jeremiah has been labeled the "weeping prophet" and, though there is hardly any Old Testament character about whom we have more biographical material, this totally unworthy phrase constitutes his entire biography for a majority of people.

He *did* weep, and good cause he had to do it. God laid on him a tremendous burden, and once when he cried out because he was carrying every bit that he possibly could God's answer to him was, "Cheer up, Jeremiah, the worst is yet to come," or, in the fine phraseology:

If thou hast run with the footmen, and they have wearied thee, then how canst thou contend with horses? and if in the land of peace, wherein thou trustedst, they wearied thee, then how wilt thou do in the swelling of Jordan?

Only a courageous spirit could stand a message like that, and Jeremiah was, on the whole, the bravest figure in the Old Testament. He was the kind of man who would have enjoyed a home, but it was denied him.

> The word of the Lord came also unto me, saying,
> Thou shalt not take thee a wife, neither shalt thou have sons or daughters in this place.

He was a priest, but he had little to do with the temple. He was a man of property, yet he encountered continuous privation. A friend of kings, he was cast into prison for reproving royalty. A stern patriot, he was under suspicion of giving aid and comfort to the enemy and was compelled at one period to take shelter with the enemy against the friends whom he had vainly sought to save. A natural optimist, loving people and desiring to be loved by them, he was forced to utter truths which estranged him from all companionship and left him a lonely outcast in a hostile land.

> Woe is me, my mother, that thou hast borne me a man of strife and a man of contention to the whole earth! I have neither lent on usury, nor

men have lent to me on usury; yet every one of them doth curse me.

Jeremiah was a countryman, born in the little town of Anathoth. When the call of God came to him to stand forth as a turbulent prophet instead of a quiet priest, it found him modest and reluctant.

> Then said I, Ah, Lord God! Behold I cannot speak: for I am a child.

The king of the country was Josiah, who meant well and tried to bring about a revival of religion. Apparently Jeremiah correctly estimated the ineffectiveness of Josiah's character and realized that the improvement was merely superficial. At any rate, he did not ally himself with the reform movement, which quickly died after the king's death. From this time on, under the driveling king Jehoiakim, Jeremiah was a stormy voice, denouncing wickedness in the nation and folly at court, and prophesying that Nebuchadnezzar would surely conquer Jerusalem. He was imprisoned. When he had written out his sermons and prophecies and was reading them at court, the king took the roll, slashed it with a pen knife and threw it into the open fire. Finally the prophet was compelled to flee with a little group of refugees into Egypt.

There the women of the company found a new fad in religion. When Jeremiah spoke to the men, saying, "Stop your wives from worshipping the moon," they bluntly refused.

> Then all the men which knew that their wives had burnt incense unto other gods . . . answered Jeremiah, saying,
>
> As for the word that thou hast spoken unto us in the name of the Lord, we will not hearken unto thee.
>
> But we will certainly do whatever thing goeth forth out of our own mouth, to burn incense unto the queen of heaven, and to pour out drink offerings unto her, as we have done, . . . for *then* had we plenty of victuals, and were well, and saw no evil.
>
> But since we left off to burn incense to the queen of heaven, and to pour out drink offerings unto her, we have wanted all things, and have been consumed by the sword and by the famine.

In other words, "The Lord doesn't look after us and the Moon does: why should we stick to the Lord?" It was the question that Jeremiah himself had to face on almost every day of his lonely, persecuted life. His Gethsemane is in chapter twenty, verses seven to nine: "O, God! I did as you told me and you didn't stand by me!" He would have liked to abandon it, but the word of the Lord was "in mine heart as a burning fire shut up in my bones." He could not escape his destiny, even though it led him over a pathway of thorns and caused him at last, according to tradition, to be stoned to death.

Baruch, his secretary, made a second copy of his biography and sermons, after the king had burned the first copy, and this, with other material which the hero worshippers of later periods added, is the book of Jeremiah that has come down to us. Baruch was faithful but disorderly or else was so pressed for time that he could not finish his work. The book is badly jumbled up, and only by following the lead of scholars can one know how to read it in order to get a clear picture. Yet even the most desultory reading reveals the majesty of the figure that stalks through its pages. No man ever spoke the truth at greater personal sacrifice. Jeremiah stood firm against the threat of the court and the anger of the crowd; noblest of all he stood firm when God himself seemed to have broken His promises and abandoned His messenger.

8. JUDAS MACCABÆUS

It is well that the list of names which our ballot brought forth should include some that are comparatively unfamiliar. For that reason, and because of his importance, as well as the inspiring character of his story, we are glad to find Judas Maccabæus well up in the list.

His record falls between the Old and the New Testaments and is told in detail in the books which formerly were printed in the Bible in slightly smaller type and called the Apocrypha. Written in Greek before the New Testament, these books were regarded as having value but a different quality from those that made up the Old Testament itself. Some of them ought still to be printed between the covers of the Bible, and none deserve to be wholly ignored.

Alexander the Great was kind enough to conquer the world at one of the easiest of all dates to remember, 333 B. C. His brilliant life went out in dissipation while he was still a very young man. When he was asked, "To whom do you leave your kingdom?" he answered, "To the strongest." Each of his four generals thought *he* was strongest, but no one was strong enough to conquer the other three. In the division which followed, Palestine was for a considerable time under the domination of Ptolemy, who ruled Egypt. He caused the Old Testament to be translated into Greek, a most wise and beneficial proceeding, for the ancient Hebrew was no longer a spoken language and most of the Jews who could read at all read Greek. So the "Septuagint," alleged to have been made by "seventy" scholars, became the Bible version mainly in use then and even in the time of Jesus.

In the subsequent redistributions of authority, Palestine passed under the domination of a Greco-Syrian dynasty, whose outstanding representative was Antiochus Epiphanes. He endeavored to unify his little empire by instituting a kind of emperor-worship, or worship of the state, and sought to superimpose this upon all the forms that were dominant in his land, especially the worship of Jehovah in the Temple at Jerusalem.

Many thousands of Jews accepted this bastard form of idolatry, including most of the priests, whose salaries went on as before. But there was one aged priest, Mattathias, who revolted and withdrew from Jerusalem to his summer home at Modin, taking with him his five sons, Jochanan, Simon, Judas, Eleazar and Jonathan. Even that retired country village was not secure from the invasion of the new paganism. To his horror, the old priest saw one of his summer neighbors come to render the detested worship, a priest of God leading him in the new idolatry. Full of wrath, the old man killed both the idolator and the priest, and he and his sons fled to the moun-

216

tains. There they rallied a band of revolution-
ists and began a series of night raids on their
enemies. They gathered strength till they were
able to meet the armies of Antiochus in open
battle, at first with no faintest hope of winning
but only with the determination to die fighting
for God and their country.

Never was a truly noble cause more valiantly
defended. In 166 B. C., Mattathias died, but
not until he had seen the struggle on the high
road to success. He counseled his sons to make
Simon their political leader and Judas their captain, and they did so.

What followed is brilliant indeed. In 164
B. C., Judas actually defeated the imperial
armies and captured Jerusalem. The Temple
was cleansed and rededicated, and the worship of
God reestablished. Judas was killed in battle in
161 B. C. The five brothers carried on in succession, each one grasping the sword as it fell
from the hand of his predecessor and while the
hilt was yet warm and the blade still red. For
more than thirty years they fought their good
fight and succeeded in giving fresh life to the
nation, establishing again a Jewish dynasty in
Jerusalem and making it possible for Jesus to
come to a people who still worshipped the God of
Abraham.

9. JOHN THE BAPTIST

If one were to seek out the most unselfish hero of history it would be difficult to name another worthy to stand even as close second to John the Baptist. He inaugurated a great movement which he might very easily have utilized for his own use; just *how* great it was we can imagine from the fact that St. Paul, coming to Ephesus a full quarter of a century after the crucifixion of Jesus, found a little group of men who were still disciples of John and knew hardly anything about Jesus. We find the same situation existing in far-away Alexandria, and we know the potency of John's name from the fact that Jesus used it in the last week of His earthly life for His own protection. The priests, His hecklers and baiters, were silent when He spoke it, fearing the people, "for all held John as a prophet."

Go back to the very beginnings of the Gospel: how did it start? By the preaching of John.

The beginning of the gospel of Jesus Christ, the Son of God;

As it is written in the prophets, Behold, I send my messenger before thy face, which shall prepare the way before thee.

The voice of one crying in the wilderness, Prepare ye the way of the Lord, make his paths straight.

John made his camp by the banks of Jordan, clothing himself in skins and eating locusts and wild honey; and there he began to announce the coming of the kingdom of heaven and to call upon men to depart from sin. How did he *know* that the kingdom of heaven was at hand? Who told him to proclaim the dawn of a new day? In what hour of the day or night does the Voice come to such a man, cutting him out from the company of his fellows, setting him apart for a lonely but majestic task? We shall never know the fullness of this mystery, but we are assured that in every age God has "left not himself without witness." To some souls in each generation He has spoken, and He still does speak.

John's success was almost instantaneous. Crowds went out from the city to attend his meetings; he became a sort of fashionable fad, attracting not only the leaders of the smart set but a sufficient number of thoughtful and important people so that even the Pharisees began to give respectful attention. One day an impressive committee went down the long winding road from Jerusalem to the Jordan, and after putting up at the most reputable tavern in the vicinity and removing the traces of their travel they waited on John in solemn array and asked him to declare whether he was the Christ, and, if not, what honorable title they might confer upon him.

> And he confessed, and denied not; but confessed, I am not the Christ.
> And they asked him, What then? Art thou Elias? And he saith, I am not. Art thou that prophet? And he answered, No.

He had his chance to claim the great place for himself and he refused it. He was only a "voice crying in the wilderness," he said, the forerunner of a Greater One to follow. He saw his own disciples go away from him to follow Jesus, and, unselfish as he was, we may be sure that it was not easy. The time came all too quickly when even his most loyal supporters recognized that his sun was being eclipsed. They resented it.

> And they came unto John, and said unto him, Rabbi, he that was with thee beyond Jordan, to whom thou bearest witness, behold, the same baptizeth, and all men come to him.
> John answered and said, . . .
> Ye yourselves bear me witness that I said, I am not the Christ, but that I am sent before him. . . .
> He must increase, but I must decrease.

Even he did not realize perhaps how fast his following would diminish, nor how soon the authorities would think it safe to seize him without precipitating a popular uprising. Suddenly he found himself in the darkness of Herod's prison, no audience there to listen to his eloquence, no contact with the outside world except through a handful of still faithful disciples. These brought him disquieting news. Jesus whom he had hailed as the Messiah, to whose upbuilding he had sacrificed every personal opportunity and interest, this Jesus was not acting the rôle of a prophet. He did not fast; He did not withdraw into the wilderness; He did not denounce men for carnal sins. On the contrary, He was feasting in the homes of publicans and proceeding happily from village to village, surrounded by laughing children and a nondescript mob of undesirables. What was He doing to bring in the kingdom? How could He carry on so cheerfully when His cousin and faithful forerunner was in the shadow of death? Was He after all the true Messiah, or had John been mistaken, his sacrifices in vain?

Tortured by such doubts, he sent two of his disciples to demand an explanation. They clambered down the rocks below the prison of Machærus by the Dead Sea and up the slope on the other side of the Jordan, and finding Jesus surrounded by enthusiastic crowds they sought a private audience and insisted on the truth.

Art thou he that should come, or do we look for another?

The inquiry must have cut Jesus to the quick. What could He answer? How could He explain to these sorrowing, reproachful messengers that their master's method was not and could not be His method? How could He make them understand that He was in truth fulfilling John's prophecy, though He remained in the happy presence of the crowd and refused to fast or denounce? He did the only thing possible; He pointed to the results, hoping that they would carry convincing testimony.

Go and shew John again those things which ye do see and hear and see:
The blind receive their sight, and the lame walk, the lepers are cleansed, and the deaf hear, the dead are raised up, and the poor have the gospel preached to them.

Did the answer satisfy John? Did he die with the inspiring assurance that his short life was in the noblest sense successful, that he had delivered his message and that it was true? Or were the agonies of doubt and discouragement his final portion?

We can never know. The end came very quickly. His head was kicked off by the toe of a dancing girl, and Jesus did not interfere to save him.

> When Jesus heard of it, he departed thence by ship unto a desert place apart.

He summoned no battalion of angels to save His friend even as, a few months later, He summoned none to save Himself. But we know what He thought of that friend:

> Verily I say unto you, Among them that are born of women there hath not risen a greater than John the Baptist.

10. SAINT PAUL

In the lists of names voted for in this series, the very highest name next only to that of Jesus was Saint Paul. Practically every ballot was marked for him, as well it might have been.

Paul was born in Tarsus, a university town in Asia Minor near the northeast corner of the Mediterranean. He knew something of classic literature and philosophy, but whether he attended the local college we do not know. He was sent by his parents, who were Jews of the strictest sect of the Pharisees, albeit his father was a free-born Roman citizen (Acts 22:24-29), to be trained by the famous teacher of the

Pharisees, Gamaliel (Acts 22:3). He was of the tribe of Benjamin, a Pharisee of the Pharisees.

We first meet him at the stoning of Stephen when he is "a young man named Saul." We last see him in prison, "Paul the aged," waiting for the sword of Nero. Unconquered by his imprisonment and peril, he towered triumphant over circumstance in the assurance that he had fought a good fight and kept the faith and finished his course.

His conversion must have followed within a few months after the stoning of Stephen. That ardent young friend of the Gentile element in the infant church left a greater successor than he could possibly have suspected in one of the men who voted for his execution. So complete is the autobiographical data in Paul's letters, and so large the imprint which he left upon the book of Acts, that we can trace almost every step of his apostolic career, and there is nowhere a more glorious record.

He was "not disobedient to the heavenly vision," says the story of his conversion. Starting to preach in a preliminary way at Damascus, he seems to have felt almost immediately the need for a quiet time when he could think things through and evolve his own message. He retired into Arabia, and we lose sight of him for three years.

> Neither went I up to Jerusalem to them which were apostles before me; but I went into Arabia, and returned again unto Damascus.
> Then after three years I went up to Jerusalem to see Peter, and abode with him fifteen days.

Almost by inadvertence he reveals the ambition which he cherished on that first visit to the capital city, that of having an honorable place in Jerusalem near the head of the apostolic group, and of his sorrowful discovery that he was *persona non grata* to the disciples and must seek a field of work afar. (Acts 22:17-21.) It must have been a heartbreaking disillusionment but it was one of the greatest blessings that ever happened to the world. For if Christianity had stayed only in Jerusalem it would hardly have survived beyond the lives of the men who saw it start.

Paul made three notable missionary journeys beyond the borders of Palestine. The first one, with Barnabas, to Cyprus and into nearer Asia Minor was in or about the years 47-48. The second, which lasted three years, 49 to 52, carried him around the end of the Mediterranean to Asia Minor, from Troas to Europe, and includes also a year and a half in Corinth. The third journey began in the autumn of 52 and extended to 56, and included a long stay at Ephesus. He was arrested in Jerusalem in April, 56, at the time of the Passover, that being his fifth visit to the city since his conversion a quarter of a century before. For two years he was in prison in Cæsarea (Acts 24:27), was nearly half a year on his way to Rome, being shipwrecked on the island of Malta and having to spend three months there, and two years in prison in relative comfort at Rome. Afterward there was apparently a release followed by another and fatal imprisonment, the loneliness of which we have a record in Second Timothy, four to six.

> For I am now ready to be offered, and the time of my departure is at hand.

We know not only where he went and what he said; we know also what he suffered.

> Of the Jews five times received I forty stripes save one.
> Thrice was I beaten with rods, once was I stoned, thrice I suffered shipwreck, a night and a day I have been in the deep;
> In journeyings often, in perils of waters, in perils of robbers, in perils by mine own country-

men, in perils by the heathen, in perils in the city, in perils in the wilderness . . .

In weariness and a painfulness, . . . in fastings often, in cold and nakedness.

What sort of a man was he who endured so much and triumphed so abundantly? He was nervous, aggressive, self-assertive, proud—a little man apparently, with weak eyes or some other physical infirmity.

Ye know how through infirmity of the flesh I preached the gospel unto you at the first.

And my temptation which was in my flesh ye despised not, nor rejected, but received me as an angel of God, even as Jesus Christ.

. . . if it had been possible ye would have plucked out your own eyes, and given them to me.

Less eloquent than Apollos, he admits frankly that his bodily presence was unimpressive and testifies to some "thorn in the flesh" that was a constant source of suffering and humiliation. He seems to have had little consciousness of natural beauties, for though he traveled through some of the finest scenery in the world there is no reference to it in his letters and no figure of speech drawn from Nature. He delighted in words of power, which recur in his letters again and again. Like Oliver Wendell Holmes, also a small man, he admired athletics, and his writings abound with references to games and contests, to fighting the good fight, and to winning the prize. Unlike the John of Revelation, he was no hater of Rome; on the contrary, he gloried in his Roman citizenship and made use of it on more than one occasion to save himself from the unjust measures of local officers.

What would the message of Jesus have become without Paul's missionary journeys and organizing ability? We can only guess the answer, but this much we know—that after about 150 A. D. Christianity nearly ceased to convert Jews and has made no notable progress in that direction since. The church in Jerusalem began to dwindle and finally faded out. But the churches which Paul planted, and the enormous momentum which his tireless energy provoked, carried forward until even the Imperial City itself was compelled to bow its proud head. Those who affirm that Paul created Christianity do him poor service, for we know how indignantly he would have denied it.

Was Paul crucified for you? or were ye baptized in the name of Paul?

I thank God that I baptized none of you, but Crispus and Gaius;

Lest any should say that I had baptized in mine own name.

He did not create Christianity, but he was the one man whose vision extended it far beyond the borders of its original home and who interpreted it in terms of world conquest. He would not be satisfied until he had seen Rome, and after that he would take the journey which he was forever talking about, "my journey into Spain." He never did make that journey. Nero blotted out the life that had achieved so mightily and that still had in its unwearied spirit the desire for so much more achievement. But the soul of the man went marching on. It carried into Spain and beyond Spain; it leaped the Atlantic and encircled the globe.

VI

TEN FAMOUS WOMEN

QUESTIONS

1. *What two women, one by a tragic exploit and the other by a memorable song about it, began a new epoch in Bible history?*
   Judges 4 and 5.

2. *What girl urged her father to fulfill his rash vow though it cost her her life?*
   Judges 11:34-36.

3. *What little girl helped a great general to recover his health?*
   II Kings 5:3.

4. *What prophetess was called into counsel when a great book was discovered?*
   II Kings 22:14.

5. *What girl danced and asked for a prophet's head in reward?*
   Matthew 14:6-11.

6. *What four women are named among the ancestors of Jesus?*
   Matthew 1:2-16.

7. *What woman warned her husband not to permit the crucifixion of Jesus?*
   Matthew 27:19.

8. *Who was the first woman in Europe to welcome the messengers of the Gospel?*
   Acts 16:14-15.

9. *What woman sat beside two judges when an apostle was on trial?*
   Acts 25:23.

10. *What advice did St. Paul give to elderly women and through them to young women?*
    Titus 2:2-5.

VI

TEN FAMOUS WOMEN

THE same letter which invited ten thousand preachers to name the ten greatest men in the Bible asked also for a list of ten famous women. Seventy-four names received votes, and the following ten are selected from among the highest, and are arranged not in the order of their popularity but in their chronological sequence.

1. Eve, "the mother of all living."
2. Ruth (who had the highest vote next to Mary, the mother of Jesus).
3. Hannah, the devoted mother.
4. The one woman whom the Bible calls great.
5. Esther, the beautiful queen.
6. Mary, the mother of Jesus (for whom practically every vote was cast).
7. Mary of Magdala.
8. The Bethany Sisters.
9. The woman of Samaria.
10. The widow who gave the mite.

1. Eve

Every ancient people has its own legend of the creation of the first man and woman, and in almost every story the woman gets the worst of it. It is only fair to Eve to remember this. Some man (Moses or another) is her biographer, and the story was written in the days when men made the rules and wrote the records in every department of life and literature.

Let us recall also, for the sake of those who insist upon the "economic interpretation" of history, that it was not a question of low wages with Eve. And for those who think that sinful people are just as sinful as they know how to be, let it be remembered that it was not the loathsome aspects of temptation that made their appeal to her but those that were rather fine and high. It is not written that "when the woman saw the fruit that it was unripe and hard and bitter and had a rotten spot in the side and a worm at the root she desired it," but

> When the woman saw that the tree was good for food, and that it was pleasant to the eyes, and a tree to be desired to make one wise, she took of the fruit thereof, and did eat, and gave also to her husband.

Bad as that incident was, there are four things to be said in palliation of Eve's offense: The fruit was good to eat—she had an eye to food values; it was pleasant to the sight—she had an esthetic nature; it was to be desired to make one wise—she was intellectually alert; she gave to her husband—she was generous.

So much for the Eve whom everybody knows, the Eve of the Garden and the transgression. We shall not linger with her. It is with Eve the girl with an unhappy memory and the swift disillusionment going forth with the young man she loved and making a home "east of Eden," whom we should like to know better. The word "east" is interesting. The whole progress of the race has been from east to west, following the sun. Go into any city and the older parts, the slums, are on the east side. There the pioneers settled and made their fortunes, and from there they were crowded westward by succeeding tides of immigrants. Eve's move was eastward instead of westward, but in all other respects she was the mother and patron saint of all those pioneer women who have followed their husbands into the new unknown. On the *May-flower,* on horseback through Cumberland Gap to the land beyond the Alleghenies and the Blue Ridge, in prairie schooner to the great open spaces, they have traveled, these pioneer women. Eve was the first of them all, carrying in her heart the haunting memory of the comforts that she continued to speak of as "back home."

With her into that home "east of Eden" went the hope of humanity. The honeymoon is over, and now it is hard work, with no small task to keep the outgo within sight of the income. The toil, the danger, the quarrels, perhaps, as to whether Adam or she was the more to blame, for who can doubt that in some moments of fatigue and discouragement such discussions did not intrude—all these made up the very human routine of her days. And the baby, Cain!

There in the backwoods is heard the lullaby of this primitive Madonna, singing the song that all mothers have sung:

> I have gotten a man
> From the Lord.

She knows very well that the child is Adam's son, and she knows Adam too well to suppose that any boy of his can be an angel; but she also knows that this child, this miracle of little pink toes and tiny hands that have such a terrible clutch at one's hair and heartstrings, is *more* than a son of Adam:

> I have gotten a man,
> *From the Lord.*

That is the theme of all cradle songs. Eve set the mothers of the world to singing. She did wrong, in that apple affair. But as a result of it she and Adam were no longer pensioners; they were working to pay off the mortgage. And weren't they happier, isn't the whole race happier, in this bustling and chaotic world than if they had stayed in Eden?

I sometimes wonder how much Eve *really* regretted!

2. RUTH

Now it came to pass in the days when the judges ruled.

Reading those first words of the book of Ruth you are tempted to skip to some other part of the Bible that gives promise of more pleasant reading. For the "days when the judges ruled" were terrible days, days of anarchy and bloodshed, of sag and reaction after a cruel war, of disorganization and uncensored living. We ourselves have lived through such a period in the World War and its aftermath. If the historian of the future were to confine his researches to the newspaper head-lines of the years 1914 to 1920, he would doubtless say, "These were times of cruelty, crime and moral break-down." Yet

THE BOOK NOBODY KNOWS

we know that underneath these superficial cur-
rents which are recorded in the head-lines there
flows the tranquil river of family life; that even
in the stormiest and most depressing eras the
great masses of common folk go quietly on,
loving each other, sacrificing for each other,
carrying forward their daily tasks in kindliness
and cheer.

So it was "in the days when the judges ruled."
The head-lines, as set forth in the book of
Judges, tell only of battle and bloodshed, intrigue and demoralization. But Ruth gives a
picture of the life of a single family and has preserved for all ages one of the most beautiful
love-stories in the world.

The story has only four chapters; you can
read it in fifteen minutes. It starts with a good
citizen named Elimelech, a resourceful man and
a loving husband and father. Because a famine
had visited his own country he migrated with his
wife, Naomi, who, like Eve, was a pioneer wife,
and his two boys, Mahlon and Chilion. The new
land offered food enough, but its climate was
somehow unkind to the visitors, for the father
died and afterward the sons also, leaving Naomi
and two beautiful young daughters-in-law,
Orpah and Ruth. Naomi's only hope was to
return to her own country, but she urged the

girls to stay behind among their friends and relatives who would look after them and doubtless provide other husbands. Orpah consented. Ruth replied in those magnificent words that have been the inspiration of so much poetry and music:

> Entreat me not to leave thee, or to return from following after thee: for whither thou goest, I will go; and where thou lodgest, I will lodge: thy people shall be my people, and thy God my God;
> Where thou diest, will I die, and there will I be buried: the Lord do so to me, and more also, if ought but death part thee and me.

So Naomi went back to Bethlehem, her old home town, and the news soon spread about that she had brought a lovely young widow with her. They were very poor, and Ruth spent her days following the reapers in the fields, for it was the law of Moses that he who owned the field should never gather quite all the crop but must leave a little in the corners that the needy might come and glean. So Ruth gleaned, and Boaz, the most desirable bachelor in Bethlehem, saw her, and the romance took place as Naomi, the shrewd old match-maker, had hoped it would.

"In the days when the judges ruled" the statesmen and the generals had their troubles, but life was not so bad a thing for simple common folk.

Have you by any chance read the genealogy of Jesus as it is given in the first chapter of Matthew? Maybe not; the long list of unfamiliar names makes a dull-looking page, but look through it some day and note an interesting fact. Mostly the names are those of men, *but there are four women.* Who are these four whose names will live forever as having passed down through their veins the blood of our Lord? A curious group.

First of all, Tamar, whose tragic story is in the thirty-eighth chapter af Genesis. Denied her lawful privilege of motherhood by the death of her husband and the failure of her husband's brother-in-law to do his duty, and by the lack of oversight and authority on the part of Judah, her father-in-law, she tricked Judah into becoming the father of her child. It was a bold and extraordinary course of action, but she took it unashamed and thus made sure that the lion-tribe of Judah should not pass away.

Rahab the harlot is second. Bath-sheba is third, that brilliant woman who abandoned Uriah the Hittite to become the favorite wife of David and the mother of Solomon.

These are the first three of the quartet, each

with a tarnished reputation but strong and self-reliant with courage to play her own part.

And the fourth ancestress of Jesus? She is Ruth, the maiden of Moab, who said, "Thy people shall be my people and thy God my God."

3. HANNAH

There is a great deal of current conversation about the "new woman" who has broken the chains of tradition and conquered kingdoms that formerly were reserved to men. In one sense this talk is all true. More women are doing more different things to-day than ever in the past, but when you have listed *all* these very modern activities you are surprised to discover that in every single one of them there was some woman of the Bible who distinguished herself thousands of years ago.

Does the modern woman write poetry? So did Deborah. Does she lead armies? Deborah did so. Does she preach? Huldah and Miriam were prophetesses. Is she a business manager? So were Abigail and Priscilla. Does she manage her house scientifically, or does she prefer rather to study and learn? Martha could probably have given her points on housekeeping, and Mary had a mind that was the pleasure and inspiration of her Lord. Human nature has not changed very much, and if you know all the people in the Bible you know at least all the *kinds* of people that there are or ever will be in the world.

Princesses and penitents, maidens and matrons of every variety, but the grandest of all are the mothers. They are on almost every page, from the mother of the sons of Noah, who gave the race its new start, to the mother of the sons of Zebedee, who petitioned that her boys might sit one on the right hand and the other on the left hand of the Master. Highest in the list of the women for whom votes were cast in our selection, greatest of all Bible mothers, excepting only Mary, the mother of Jesus, is an old-fashioned Old Testament woman named Hannah, who named her first son

Samuel, saying, Because I have asked him of the Lord.

Like Samson, who was born a little earlier and whose story is part and parcel of the tale of heroes, Samuel was dedicated for a great work. While he was yet a little lad, Hannah sent him to school to Eli, the grand old priest of Shiloh.

And she said [to Eli] . . . I am the woman that stood by thee here, praying . . .

> For this child I prayed; and the Lord hath
> given me my petition. . . .
> Therefore also I have lent him to the Lord; as
> long as he liveth he shall be lent to the Lord.

So Samuel grew up, as Eli's own sons did
not, with a hunger for knowledge and a devotion to duty which made him the strongest
constructive force in his generation. Every
year Hannah went up to Shiloh to visit him,
and every year she made him a "little coat."
There is something in those words that reaches
down and grips your heartstrings. You can
picture the year-long care and yearning affection
that went into that little garment. She did not
buy the cloth and sew it up; she sheared and
washed and dyed the wool, and carded and spun
and wove it. She had to guess at the size, and
you can see her going about to all the women of
the neighborhood who had sons a year older than
her own son had been when she last had seen him.
Then she measured her own absent boy with a
mother's imagination and cut the cloth to that
measurement. And every year the coat was
larger. Her boy, her own Samuel, was growing
up, strong and tall, and would be a great man
some day.

It all came true. The son of such a mother
could hardly fail to be great. Samson had won

sporadic victories and failed through lack of moral purpose. Samuel became priest, circuit judge, president of the school of the prophets, and guide to those who led armies, and in every one of those relations he was a dominant figure. He became a state-builder and a king-maker. He stood in the gap during the transition from semi-anarchy to settled government. He practically wrote the constitution for the permanent rulership of Israel in the day of its kings.

Now and then as he rode on his circuit, holding court, opening religious festivals, organizing movements for sanitation and better government, he passed through the hill country of Ephraim, and a little woman back in the crowd saw him presiding and directing, and said, "That is my boy up there." And when it came to pass, as it did, that people said of Saul or of David, "He never could have been so great a man but for Samuel," there was a woman whose heart gave a great leap.

For Samuel himself could never have been so great a man if it had not been for Hannah.

4. THE ONE WOMAN WHOM THE BIBLE CALLS GREAT

Ask a dozen Bible students, "Who is the one woman whom the Bible calls great?" and even they would likely give a wide variety of answers. Was it Pharaoh's daughter, whose wit and courage saved the life of Moses? Was it the mighty Queen of Sheba, ruler of an empire? Was it the mother of Solomon, who made him king, or the mother of John the Baptist, who consecrated him to his splendid mission? None of these; none of the women of royal birth; none whose close relation to kings or apostles made their names famous for deeds of public renown. Quite a different sort of woman altogether. Let us look a moment at the picture of her which is given in the fourth chapter of Second Kings.

First of all, she was domestic, a home-maker, living not in the city but in one of the northern villages. Her husband was a farmer, which meant that he had his house on the edge of town, as was the custom then. A main road ran near by, and important people used it. Solomon appears to have traveled there in his time and to have seen a pretty girl whom he desired for his harem, but her heart remained true to her shepherd love. That girl, too, was a person of note, and we have the story of her temptation and her unpurchasable love in the "Song of Songs." She perhaps deserved to be called great, but it is not for her either that the Bible reserves its finest title.

The "great woman" had executive ability. In the early days of her married life she had no children, and that fact shadowed her life. But she did not complain. The narrative distinctly implies that she accepted the situation and made the best of it, giving herself to such activities as lightened the load of her husband. She was religious, and she was hospitable. To these last two characteristics she owed the friendship that brought her the happiness which she desired above all else, and won for her the place of honor in the Bible records.

> And it fell on a day, that Elisha passed to Shunem, where was a great woman; and she constrained him to eat bread. And so it was, that as oft as he passed by, he turned in thither to eat bread.
>
> And she said unto her husband, Behold now, I perceive that this is an holy man of God, which passeth by us continually.
>
> Let us make a little chamber, I pray thee, on the wall; and let us set for him there a bed, and a table, and a stool, and a candlestick: and it shall be, when he cometh to us, that he shall turn in thither.

As to what happened afterward, the fulfillment of her long desire for a son, the growth of the boy, his illness, and his miraculous recovery at the hand of the prophet Elisha—all these are written in the next thirty verses of the chapter. They are well worth reading, but what most concerns us has already been related. She was just a small-town woman who loved her husband and wanted motherhood more than anything else in the world, and baked good bread and kept a clean guest room. The Bible does not tell us her name, but of all the women whose biographies it records it speaks of her alone as "great."

5. ESTHER

Many eminent scholars tell us that the book of Esther and the book of Daniel are two splendid pieces of propaganda, written to lift the spirits of the Jews in their days of exile and spur them on to daring deeds. If this be true, the knowledge detracts nothing from our pleasure in the two books, or from their value for the purposes for which they were written. Both are thrilling narratives, and no figure stands out more life-like than that of Esther, the favorite of the harem, who by her courage saved her people.

The story comes late in the Old Testament chronology, dealing with the period when there were numerous Jews in Mesopotamia, descendants of those who were carried away captive by Nebuchadnezzar in 586 B. C. A hundred years

had passed and, while many Jews had returned
to Palestine, others were settled in different
parts of the big unwieldy Persian kingdom,
ruled over by Ahasuerus

> which reigned, from India even unto Ethiopia,
> over an hundred and seven and twenty provinces.

The Jews in his reign suffered no political dis-
abilities, and one of them, Mordecai, had become
prime minister.

He was plotted against by a politician named
Haman, who through misrepresentation got
Mordecai discharged and caused the king to pro-
mulgate a decree of massacre against the Jews.
It was at this crisis that Mordecai went to
Esther, demanding

> that she should go in unto the king, to make sup-
> plication unto him, and to make request before him
> for her people.

She replied that no one was permitted to approach the king without being sent for by name
and that the penalty of disobedience was death.
In noble words Mordecai argued the case, and at
length Esther was persuaded.

> Go, gather together all the Jews that are pres-
> ent in Shushan [she replied], and fast ye for me,
> and neither eat nor drink three days, night or day:

I also and my maidens will fast likewise; and so
will I go in unto the king, which is not according to
the law: and if I perish, I perish.

The third day came. Modestly but with firm
step and head erect, she moved into the inner
court where sat Ahasuerus on his mighty throne.
There was an awful moment of suspense while
the courtiers watched with bated breath to see
what destruction would descend upon this girl
who had dared to break the law. But her beauty
was irresistible. The king held out his scepter,
the sign of royal recognition. Esther knelt and
touched it and made her plea and won.

The wicked decree was revoked; the Jews
were restored to favor and began promptly to
take advantage of their opportunities to grow
rich. Haman by poetic justice was hanged on
the high gallows which he had built for Mordecai.
As for Esther, her name became imperishably
glorious, the Joan of Arc of the Old Testament,
the woman who dared and triumphed when the
men of the nation were at their wits' ends.

The finest passage in the whole book is
Mordecai's ringing answer to Esther when she
hesitated to approach the king, arguing that her
feeble strength and abilities could not possibly
prevail in such an emergency:

THE BOOK NOBODY KNOWS

Then Mordecai commanded to answer Esther, Think not with thyself that thou shalt escape in the king's house, more than all the Jews.

For if thou altogether holdest thy peace at this time, then shall there enlargement and deliverance arise to the Jews from another place; but thou and thy father's house shall be destroyed: *and who knoweth whether thou art come to the kingdom for such a time as this?*

Those words have rung down the corridors of Time as an undying challenge to the courage and faith of youth. "Let no faint-heartedness turn you aside from the duty to which you are clearly called, no matter how hard that duty may be or how much apparently beyond your powers. If you fail some one else will do the job and win the glory. 'Enlargement and deliverance will arise . . . from another place.' But you will have been untrue to your calling, for how do you know but what you were sent into the world for this special duty at this special time?"

. . . and who knoweth whether thou art come to the kingdom for such a time as this?

6.   Mary, the Mother of Jesus

We who call ourselves Protestants have been almost rude in our attitude toward the mother

250

of Jesus. What beauty of face and figure there must have been in her whose own blood nourished and whose own body shaped the little hands and feet, the heart and brain of Jesus of Nazareth! What elevation in the mind that could conceive and chant the Magnificat!

> . . . My soul doth magnify the Lord,
> And my spirit hath rejoiced in God my Saviour.
> For he hath regarded the low estate of his handmaiden: for, behold, from henceforth all generations shall call me blessed.
> For he that is mighty hath done to me great things; and holy is his name.
> And his mercy is on them that fear him from generation to generation.

Finish the reading of that great hymn of praise as Luke records it in his first chapter. Look in your reference Bible at the little index letters sprinkled through the text and the corresponding letters in the margin. Note that the beginning of the Magnificat is reminiscent of Hannah's rejoicing over the prospect of the birth of Samuel, and that almost every phrase suggests a possible source in historic records. This young woman, sixteen or seventeen perhaps, had read the literature of her nation and had made it her own. Her mind and spirit were richly stored. Reverence, gratitude, high spirituality, and great sympathy with the common lot of humanity are in the Magnificat. Socialists and other champions of human rights have claimed to find in it the possible source of Jesus' sympathy with the poor.

Motherhood is the most expensive of all earth's luxuries, and being the mother of the Messiah was a costly privilege. Think what it meant to Mary to have to go into Egypt and remain there while Joseph, resourceful and strong though he was, struggled to support the family. How her heart must have yearned for her home and girlhood friends. Think of the bewildering problems and perplexities of having a Son grow up with ambitions and expressions which she and Joseph could only dimly apprehend. She knew in the utmost degree the wonder and the worry, the high hope and the deep concern of all the mothers of geniuses.

And they [Mary and Joseph] understood not the saying which he [Jesus] spake unto them. .· . . but his mother kept all these sayings in her heart.

Doubtless the family had to practise self-denial in order that Jesus might have time for study. Doubtless she was often disturbed by His dreamy absorption in ideas, His apparent lack of interest in what they should eat, what they should drink and wherewithal they should be clothed, though after Joseph's death He took up the burden of family support and carried it nobly until the younger children were old enough to stand alone. It was not merely as the "carpenter's son" but as "the carpenter" that He was known.

There were times when she was troubled about Him; times when she wondered whether He could be quite right in His mind; times, like that awful day of His visit to Nazareth, when her spirit must have been rent asunder by fear of the forces which were arrayed against Him and a tragic premonition of what these would finally accomplish against her beloved Son. Yet troubled, and even doubting, she did not surrender. Of those who stood firm at the end, a large proportion were women, and she leads them all. Hanging there in agony upon the cross, He gave His last thought to her future safety and comfort.

Now there stood by the cross of Jesus, his mother . . .

When Jesus therefore saw his mother, and the disciple standing by, whom he loved, he saith unto his mother, Woman behold thy son!

Then saith he to the disciple, Behold thy

mother! And from that hour that disciple [John] took her unto his own home.

We are not given the record of her later years, but they must have been beautiful in faith and self-sacrifice, for the devotion of those members of the early church grew constantly more tender and their reverence more exalted. Only a beautiful spirit could have inspired such adoration. She is nobler, beyond comparison, than any of the other women of the Bible, and the women on the whole stand higher in the splendor of their faith than the men. Not one unworthy woman appears in the tragedy of the crucifixion.

> Not she with traitorous kiss her Saviour stung;
> Not she denied Him with unholy tongue:
> She when apostles shrank could danger brave—
> Last at the cross and earliest at the grave.

7. MARY OF MAGDALA

The name Mary was immensely popular in the time of Jesus because of the love of the Jewish people for Mariamne, the Jewish wife of Herod, who was murdered by him. Hence there are so many women in the New Testament named Mary that we sometimes find it difficult to keep track of them. Foremost, of course, is

Mary, the mother of Jesus. Next in order of her importance is Mary of Magdala. Of her early history we know nothing except that she suffered with some nervous or mental complaint.

> And it came to pass afterward, that he went throughout every city and village, preaching and shewing the glad tidings of the kingdom of God; and the twelve were with him.
>
> And certain women, which had been healed of evil spirits and infirmities, Mary called Magdalene, out of whom went seven devils.

Just what the "seven devils" were we are not told. The phrase has been assumed to mean that Mary was immoral, and for this reason prostitutes are often called Magdalenes. We have no proof either for or against this assumption, just as there is no evidence that Mary was "the woman in the city, which was a sinner," who washed the feet of Jesus with precious ointment at the feast in the Pharisee's house. If Mary *was* this humble and tearful woman, then noble indeed was her repentance. But inasmuch as definite evidence against her is altogether lacking, the world has been less than generous in so easily passing judgment; certainly her subsequent career proved her to be one of the grandest characters in Bible history.

Magdala is a town of Galilee, situated not far from Capernaum and Bethsaida on the Galilean lake. There Mary spent her girlhood; there she suffered the mental calamity which befell her, and, if with the clouded mind came also the clouded reputation, we need not wonder at that. But her faith in Jesus restored her reason, and her sins, whatever they were, were forgiven.

We know the names of a few of the women who followed Jesus on that last journey from Galilee to Jerusalem and "ministered to him of their substance." Three of them were Marys. Some apprehension or expectation of crisis, some woman's instinct caused them to leave their homes and be His companions in this last stage of His public work. They were in the pitiful little procession that followed along the Sorrowful Way, and they were present also at the crucifixion. Possibly if we knew all the truth we should find there were five instead of three, the other two being Mary of Bethany and Mary the mother of Mark in whose home the Last Supper was held. We are confident it was this Mary who was hostess of our Lord and His disciples at the Last Supper, and whose large upper room became the habitual meeting-place of the disciples, because, when Peter was released from prison, and sought at once his fellow disciples, he went to the place where they were accustomed to gather and it was the house of Mary, the mother of Mark. (Acts 12:12.) Her name appears but seldom, but her hospitality gave the infant church a home. She, also, and quite possibly Mary of Bethany, were there in the sorrowful procession of the cross. But we are not sure of the five. We know that there were three Marys there, and Mary of Magdala was one of them.

"Crucified, dead and buried!" Terrible words. The apostolic group was stunned and paralyzed. How the eleven disciples spent the hours from nightfall of Friday till dawn of Sunday, we do not know. But on Easter morning, "while it was yet dark" (John 20:1) these women who had seen Jesus crucified came with spices to anoint His body. They did not know that Joseph of Arimathæa and Nicodemus had already performed that melancholy service and that Jesus had been buried with an hundred weight of spices, a prince's burial (John 19:38-42). They reached the tomb, wondering who would roll away the stone for them, and behold, it was already rolled away. And the angel said, "He is not here; He is risen." The others hurried back to tell the disciples, but Mary "stood without, weeping." She it was who first saw the Lord.

No wonder Renan, skeptic as he was, marveled at the faith which caused her to see that vision of a living Christ and to proclaim it. He had a skeptic's easy explanation, but he said that no sane person ever saw anything that gave to the world such comfort as the vision of love that the Magdalene beheld. Peter and John ran to the sepulchre and found the empty tomb; the whole city knew of it before night and wondered what had become of the body. But Mary's eyes first beheld Him and her glad voice first told the incredulous disciples. In the power of her faith and the blessing of her good tidings only Mary the mother of Jesus deserves to stand before this other beautiful and devoted follower of Jesus, Mary of Magdala.

8. THE BETHANY SISTERS

They lived a little way out of Jerusalem in a sheltered suburban home which Jesus loved to visit for refreshment and rest. One of them, Martha, was the practical housekeeper; the other, Mary, had the soul of a dreamer and the eyes of faith. Down through the ages the sons and daughters of these two have come; the sons of Martha, careful for many things and good things at that; the sons of Mary, listening to the

Word and treasuring it in their hearts. Kipling
has dramatized them for us:

> And the sons of Mary smile and are blest;
>   They know that the angels are on their side;
> They know that in them is the grace confessed,
>   And for them are the mercies multiplied.
> They sit at the feet; they hear the Word;
>   They see how surely the promise runs:
> They have cast their burden upon the Lord,
>   And the Lord, He lays it on Martha's sons.

Martha was not lacking in faith. Hers was
one of the most beautiful of all confessions.
Jesus asked her if she believed in a doctrine, and
she said, "Yes, Lord; that is to say, I believe in
you." (John 11:27.) As for the theology of
it, she was bewildered. Her brother was dead;
she did not see any way out of that sorrow, but
she believed in Jesus, and He accepted that
faith at its full value. Millions of people who
are perplexed by the creeds ought to read the
story of Martha and be comforted. She fretted
once when she ought not to have done so (Luke
10:38-42), but when the test came she had a
vital faith, even though she did not understand
the creeds.

But Mary's was the inventive love that knew
how to do the unusual thing and do it beautifully.

Then Jesus six days before the Passover came to Bethany, where Lazarus was which had been dead, whom he raised from the dead.

There they made him a supper; and Martha served: but Lazarus was one of them that sat at the table with him.

Then took Mary a pound of ointment of spikenard, very costly, and anointed the feet of Jesus, and wiped his feet with her hair: and the house was filled with the odour of the ointment.

Then said one of his disciples, Judas Iscariot, Simon's son, which should betray him,

Why was not this ointment sold for three hundred pence, and given to the poor?

This he said, not that he cared for the poor; but because he was a thief, and had the bag, and bare what was put therein.

Then said Jesus, Let her alone: against the day of my burying hath she kept this.

For the poor always ye have with you; but me ye have not always.

Her love was prophetic. She had no inside knowledge of the plots to kill Jesus. She simply had apprehension of coming evil and she knew that the time to do the beautiful thing is now, "against my burial." When Jesus was dead no one of the disciples would have grudged the alabaster box, but He needed that fragrance while He lived.

Much of our extravagance at funerals is horrible, not because of the waste, for love demands an expression beyond the calculation of cold economy, but because it mocks the penuriousness of the years that have gone before. Mary knew that the time to be extravagant is when love can express itself in an appeal to life and not in a costly and useless libation after death. So she made her gift of three hundred pence, a year's wages for a working man of those days, and Jesus said:

> Verily I say unto you, Wheresoever this gospel shall be preached in the whole world, there shall also this, that this woman hath done, be told for a memorial of her.

He never said that of the deed of any man.

9. THE WOMAN OF SAMARIA

The whole community first to hear attentively the message of Jesus was neither Nazareth nor Jerusalem. The place of His youth cast Him out, and the city that should have enthroned Him sent Him to the cross. The first city where Jesus was received and acknowledged was Sychar, a village in Samaria, close by Jacob's well.

It is historic ground. The two mountains of Ebal and Gerezim stand over against each other with a narrow valley between, and the caravans and foot travelers go that way. In ancient times the patriarch, Jacob, dug a well there, and he and his family and flocks found refreshment. That well is still in existence. Upon its curb one day sat Jesus. It is the one spot on earth where we can locate to a square yard just where He sat or stood. He sat there, tired and thirsty.

A Samaritan woman came to draw water, and He asked her for a drink. It would seem to have been a common enough courtesy, but it surprised her. It was true then and still is that the "Jews have no dealings with the Samaritans." In the city called Nablous, the ancient Shechem, of which Sychar is a kind of detached suburb, is still a little Samaritan colony. Its people and the Jews have no contacts. The Samaritans still are ready to argue that in their synagogue is the one true place of worship. They say, "Here is where the body of Joseph is buried, and with it the bodies of the other patriarchs. Why are none of them in Jerusalem? Because Jerusalem is a recent thing, the capital of David but not of the ancient patriarchs. Our temple is older than that in Jerusalem. Here the Law was ratified. Here is Mount Gerezim, the holy mountain. This is the one true shrine of God."

Nothing in the life of Jesus is more impressive than His enormous care for and sublime faith in the individual. Most reformers, impressed with the great responsibilities of their mission and the shortness of human life, have been busy, preoccupied, hard to get at. They have been "in conference," they have worked on schedule; you might see them perhaps for ten minutes a week from Wednesday but you must see their secretaries first and make an appointment. Jesus had only three short years in which to speak His message and train up a group of followers who could carry on. From the hour when John the Baptist gave up his life in Herod's prison the shadow of the cross fell dark across His path; He knew that the end was inevitable and could not possibly be far off. Yet he allowed Himself to be constantly interrupted, much to the impatience of the disciples, and of Judas in particular. Little children flocked about Him, and the disciples tried to hold them off. He rebuked their efficient efforts to protect His time and conserve His strength.

> Suffer little children to come unto me, and forbid them not: for of such is the Kingdom of Heaven.

He had time to attend feasts and social parties. On His last journey to Jerusalem, carrying as

He did the burden and anxiety of the whole human race, He was not too busy to turn aside at the cry of a single blind beggar. And He did not hesitate, at that well in Samaria, to impart the most sublime truth of His whole ministry to an audience of one, a Samaritan woman.

> The hour cometh, and now is, when the true worshipers shall worship the Father in spirit and in truth: for the Father seeketh such to worship him.
>
> God is a spirit: and they that worship him must worship him in spirit and in truth.

The Samaritan woman believed the message, the truth which He had never before spoken to any one and was not to tell to His own disciples until some weeks afterward. He was the Christ, but the Christ of the Samaritans as well as of the Jews, of all peoples everywhere, regardless of boundary, regardless of racial or religious traditions, transcending all barriers and all ritual and forms.

> And upon this came his disciples, and marvelled that he talked with the woman: yet no man said, What seekest thou? or, Why talkest thou with her?
>
> The woman then left her water-pot, and went her way into the city, and saith to the men,
>
> Come, see a man, which told me all things that ever I did: is not this the Christ?
>
> Then they went out of the city, and came unto him.

Her neighbors, too, believed, first because of her testimony and then because their own hearts told them that He spoke the truth. Thus was the first community on earth evangelized, with the Christian message. Who carried the message? A woman who had not been by any means what society terms a "good woman," but who was kind enough to do a kindness to a Jew in giving him a cup of water and who received from Him in turn, and passed on to others, a drink of the water of life.

10. THE WIDOW WHO GAVE THE MITE

Reckoning up the great givers of the world, the Carnegies with their libraries, the Rockefellers with their universities, the Smithsons with their gifts to learning and research, the builders of hospitals, and the doers of great deeds of mercy, whose name stands as the one whose gift has produced more hard cash than any other? Without question it is the widow who gave the mite. As is usual where women play a part in the narrative, it is Luke who tells this story (21:1-40).

The scene took place on Tuesday in Holy Week, and rather late in the afternoon. It had been a day of controversy, and Jesus, wearied and rejected, was leaving the temple. He and

His disciples had been within the third court.
The first was the court of the Gentiles, where
any well-behaved person might go unhindered.
The next was the court of the women, so called
not because it was exclusively for women but
because it was as far as women were permitted
to go. The next was the inner court, the Court
of Israel, as far as a layman could approach.
Beyond that was the Holy Place, where only the
priests had admission, and still beyond, the Holy
of Holies, where the High Priest went once a
year. Jesus and His disciples were all laymen;
there was not a priest among them. They went
to the inner court but not into the Holy Place,
much less into the Holy of Holies. And as they
withdrew they passed through the court of the
women. There were thirteen chests around the
walls, with gold-plated trumpets into which con-
tributions were dropped. The feasts brought
many pious Jews from a distance, and this was
the place where they made their offerings.

Many that were rich cast in much.

There came a poor widow, slipping silently to
a trumpet-throated receptacle near a corner, and
cast in two copper coins so small in value that
we have to reckon in mills to get an approach to
an equivalent.

266

Obligation is commensurate with ability. From the throne of God down to the depth of the lowest hell there is one rule—every moral being is under bond to do his best. God being perfect in goodness is no better than a good God ought to be. "Be ye therefore perfect, even as your Father in heaven is perfect" means no more nor no less than this, that God does His best and we ought to do ours. Christ's gift of Himself on the cross was not more than Christ ought to have done. "Ought not the Christ to have suffered?" Certainly, if by so doing He could save the world. Even Christ did no more than the Son of God ought to have done. In some way we must do our best or we fall below God's measure and the measure of our own conscience. The poor widow gave her all.

And she has inspired millions and millions of people who, except for her, would have thought their gift too small or have measured it by too unworthy a unit of devotion. If we were to reckon up the sums that have been given for charitable causes by reason of her gift we should know that she was first among all philanthropists. We do not need to reduce the words of Jesus to cold arithmetical prose, but if we insist on that still it is true.

This poor widow hath cast in more than they all.

VII
HOW DID WE GET THE BIBLE?

QUESTIONS

Can you answer these questions? The **answers are** all in this chapter.

1. *How many books does the Bible quote or refer to that have perished?*
2. *What language did Jesus speak?*
3. *What is the Apocrypha?*
4. *When were the last Old Testament books admitted to the Canon?*
5. *What great scholar went to Bethlehem, lived there for years and made a noble translation of the Bible which is still used by a large section of the Christian Church?*
6. *What is "lower criticism"? "Higher criticism"?*
7. *What are the three most famous Bible manuscripts owned by the Roman Catholic, the Greek and the Protestant Churches, and where are they?*
8. *What English scholar was forced to flee from his native land and was afterward arrested and killed for translating the Bible into English?*
9. *What English king encouraged the making of a translation of the Bible into English?*

How Did We Get the Bible?

WHILE these chapters were appearing in serial form a surgeon of national reputation sent this request:

"Before you finish your story of *The Book,* please be sure to give us the answer to these two questions:

"1. How were the books of the Bible gathered into a collection and distinguished as a group by themselves? Who selected them, and how do we know that the right ones were selected?

"2. By what means were these chosen books preserved and handed down? Who decided that they ought to be translated into modern languages and who did the translating?"

Let us deal first with the Old Testament. It would be very pleasant if we could say that some one group of men, meeting in Jerusalem about 400 B. C., selected the books which we now have and certified for all time that these and no others should be the Old Testament. But such is not the case. As the writing of these books was an evolution, so was their selection. Largely, they have been preserved to us by the process known as the survival of the fittest.

The ancient Hebrews held many other books in high regard, of which nearly thirty are referred to in the Old Testament. Twenty-four of these are sunk beyond all knowledge. The story about the sun standing still for Joshua is quoted from an old book of war songs known as the Book of Jasher or the Book of the Just (Joshua 10:13). David's "Song of the Bow" (II Samuel 1:18) is from the same book, but except for these fragments the Book of the Just has perished. So also has another old song book, The Book of the Wars of the Lord, of which we have a fragment in the twenty-first chapter of Numbers, fourteenth verse. The books of Kings are largely compiled from more extended records, which sometimes are referred to by name:

> Now the rest of the acts of Jeroboam, and all that he did, and his might, how he warred, and how he recovered Damascus, and Hamath, which belonged to Judah, for Israel, are they not written in the book of the chronicles of the kings of Israel?

This is not the book of Chronicles that we have, which was written long after the book of Kings;

the citation is to a book which has been lost for centuries.

We see, then, that the Old Testament is the surviving portion of a much larger number of books. It does not comprise sacred as opposed to secular books, but is the whole body of ancient Hebrew literature now extant. Philo, an Alexandrian Jew who lived in the second century before the Christian era, gives a list of books nearly identical with those we have but omits seventeen that are in our list. Jesus, the son of Sirach, closely parallels our list but does not stop with it. He recognizes the work of a contemporary, Simon, as worthy to be included and, what is rather remarkable, he thinks his own book good enough to be a part of the Bible. In the latter case his judgment is probably right. His book, Ecclesiasticus, is a noble and worthy religious poem, and we are poorer for having dropped it from our Bible with the rest of the Apocrypha. Josephus, the great Jewish historian, does not name the books of the Old Testament, but he limits the period of their production to the end of the Persian rule and gives the number as twenty-two, the number of letters in the Hebrew alphabet. This was counting the five books of Moses one, the twelve minor prophets one, and certain other combinations.

No two of these authorities precisely agreed, but two processes tended to fix the selection. First was the fact that Hebrew became a dead language four centuries before Christ, and was succeeded by Aramaic, a language about as much like Hebrew as German is like English. Jesus, we know, spoke Aramaic. The name for God which he taught, *Abba,* father, was Aramaic. His words on the cross, *Eloi, Eloi, Lama sabachthani,* were Aramaic. He did not speak Hebrew, though He probably could read it, as it was the language of the synagogue scrolls, and we know he could read those (Luke 4:17). But what He read was His nation's classic tongue and not His native speech. Parts of Daniel, a very late book, and one or two bits in the minor prophets are in Aramaic, but in general the Old Testament books that survived were in the old classic Hebrew. Those that bore a later stamp were received with suspicion, if at all.

The other factor which tended to fix a canon, or acknowledged body of books, was the translation of the Old Testament into Greek by a group of scholars whose work began under Ptolemy, King of Egypt, about two centuries before Christ. In this translation, called the Septuagint, or work of seventy scholars, was included a body of sacred literature already in

Greek, the books known to us as the Apocrypha. These were a part of the Bible of Jesus and the apostles and were, of course, held sacred, as were also certain books from which the New Testament quotes, but which have not come down to us. The Apocalypse of Enoch is an example. Jude quotes it in the first chapter of his little epistle, the fourteenth verse.

Thus, while certain books from the ancient Hebrew had come to be accepted before the time of Jesus as entitled to special reverence, the fringes and margins of that collection were still open to dispute and were, in fact, disputed vigorously for two hundred years. For instance, a very early bishop of Sardis who made a journey to Palestine for the express purpose of learning, if he could, precisely what books the Jews accepted as canonical, omitted Esther, Ezra and Lamentations from his list. And the question of whether the two books, Ecclesiastes and the Song of Songs, should be accounted sacred was not settled until the Council of Jamnia, about 90 A. D.

We may sum it all up by saying that the ancient books which were most used and gave most inspiration survived and, by being translated, secured a place for themselves in the canon. These include an out-and-out love song which has no religious motive; a book which does not mention the name of God, and another, Ecclesiastes, which is very contradictory. But the selection, made by the process of survival and on the basis of those books which were best beloved, is probably much finer that it would have been if a group of men, however devoted, had set themselves at any one time to assume the whole responsibility.

So much for the Old Testament. How were the New Testament books selected? Again, by the process of use.

The first books, "read in churches" with the Old Testament selections, were apostolic letters, notably those of Paul, and including generally, though not invariably, the longer epistles of John, Peter and James. When the Gospels appeared they were immediately used in like fashion, and at once assumed a place of priority, not because any one in authority said it must be so but because they were so important and so interesting. For a good while there was no attempt to make complete collections. Few churches had all the New Testament books and many had other books, as the Epistle of Clement and the Shepherd of Hermas, which were loved.

When discussion began as to which books ought to be read regularly, there was immediate agreement on the most important ones, the four Gospels and the larger epistles. There was a good deal of doubt about Revelation and Second Peter and the two short epistles of John, which were relatively unimportant, as was then acknowledged and is still evident. But gradually there came to be agreement, not by authority but by the test of general usage, and the translation, and later the printing of the Bible, finally fixed the list.

If any one asks whether we know absolutely that every book in the Old and New Testaments is holy above all other books, the answer is, We do not. No one can say that Esther, which is in the Bible, is nobler than Ecclesiasticus, which has been dropped out; certainly it is not so religious or so sweet in its spirit. No one can say that the Epistle of Jude is more inspired than the Epistle of Clement. The mountain range of the Bible shades off into foot-hills, and we do not know just where the range begins or ends. But the range is there, towering magnificently above all other literature. Scholars may discuss its measurements and limits; the theologically minded may battle over its "inspiration." Let them argue. What the world needs is fewer folk to argue and a whole lot more to read.

We come now to the second question, How were these chosen books preserved through the ages and passed down to us?

Until the invention of printing, which was desired mainly that the Bible might be published, copies were made by hand, and errors inevitably crept in, no matter how scrupulous the copyists' care. Hence in making translations it became desirable to have as many of them for comparison as possible. The earliest manuscript copies that have survived to our time date from the fourth century A. D., and the story of one of them, the Sinaitic, will illustrate the vicissitudes through which they have passed.

On March 24, 1844, a German scholar, Lobegott Freidrich Konstantin Tischendorf, arrived at St. Catherine's monastery on the Sinaitic peninsula. His name, Lobegott, "Praise God," had been given to him by his mother who, having a presentiment that her child would be born blind, cried out her joy when she discovered that his eyes were all right. "Lobegott!" she exclaimed. His two eyes needed to be very keen, for his business as a scholar was to search for old manuscripts and examine them. On this particular trip he had been through the libraries of Alexandria and Cairo, as well as the convents of the Greek and Armenian cnurches, without success. His visit to St. Catherine's monastery was in the nature of a last hope, for it was known that a rich library had been preserved there through the ages and was now, in the nineteenth century, curiously unappreciated by the monks.

Lobegott was given free access to the library, but he did not at first discover anything of value. In the evening, however, a strange thing occurred. There was sent up to his room as kindling for the fire a basket containing some leaves of an old manuscript, which he examined. To his amazement he found a number of bits of the Old Testament in Greek. His cry of astonishment ought to have been repressed, for the monks took quick note of it. Although two similar lots of leaves had already been burned, the monks, when they heard his exclamation, immediately became jealous for the portions which remained. With great difficulty Lobegott secured permission to take back to Leipsic forty-seven leaves. They proved to be part of one of the oldest Greek manuscripts of the Old Testament in existence.

Immediately, the eager scholar set to work through an influential friend to secure the rest of the volume, but the monks had learned its value and would not give it up. In 1853, he

went back to the convent and was welcomed, but
could not find a trace of the lost parchment.
But in 1859, he returned for a third time, having now the authority of the Czar of Russia, for
the convent was Greek and the Czar was the
head of the Greek Church. Many valuable
manuscripts were placed in his hands, some of
which he had not seen on either of his previous
visits, but the chief treasure had disappeared as
completely as if the earth had swallowed it up.
Sorrowfully, he prepared to depart. On his
last evening he walked with the steward of the
convent in the garden and was invited to his
room for refreshment. As they sat together at
the table, the steward said casually, "I, too, have
a copy of the Septuagint," and took down and
untied a parcel wrapped in red cloth.

Imagine the almost delirious joy of Lobegott
when he saw not only the Old Testament pages
he had glimpsed in 1844, but the New Testament complete! It was one of the most thrilling
moments in the history of patient, scientific research, and a vital moment to the whole Christian
world, for it gave us one of the oldest, finest and
most accurate of all Biblical manuscripts. For
a half-century this so-called Sinaitic has been
in the library of Petrograd, the chief literary
treasure of the Greek Church.

HOW DID WE GET THE BIBLE?

There are only a few of these extremely old manuscripts, and the three most precious of them are this Sinaitic, the Vatican at Rome, and the Alexandrine, presented to Charles I of England in 1628 and placed in the British Museum upon its establishment in 1753. It is interesting that of the three finest Bible records one is in the possession of Protestants, one of Roman Catholics and one of the Greek Church. Each sect is most generous in permitting the use of its treasure by scholars of all Christian communions, while taking the utmost care to preserve it.

There are, of course, thousands of fragments of the Bible or parts of it of more or less value. Among these are certain "palimpsests," or manuscripts, which later fell into the hands of those who wanted the parchment for other purposes and erased the Bible text and wrote other books instead. Chemical processes have been used to restore the Bible text, and in some instances valuable readings have been discovered.

This recital of the way in which manuscripts have been found brings us to the mention of a class of men of whom the average layman knows very little, and most of that little is wrong. These are the Biblical critics. "Criticizing the Bible!" What columns of rhetoric have been printed, what floods of oratory have been poured out by those who could not have told, to save their souls, what a Biblical critic is or what he does.

There are two kinds of Biblical critics: the lower or textual critics, and the higher or literary critics. The terms lower and higher do not mean that one group claims or is admitted to be more important than the other, much less that there is an assumption of arrogance on the part of those that are "higher," but that one kind of study follows and is built upon the other.

The lower critic is a man of technical skill in the deciphering of ancient texts and manuscripts. He has critical ability, that is, the ability to judge critically, for criticism is nothing more or less than the science of correct judgment. To the average layman a manuscript of the fourteenth century may seem as ancient as one of the fourth. It may be more soiled and show greater sign of age. But the critic does not look simply at the wear and stain. He is a judge of parchments, of methods of tanning skins, of kinds of ink, of styles of making letters. He distinguishes between "uncial" and "cursive" Greek; between "pointed" and "unpointed" Hebrew.

These lower critics are not widely known;

they are not highly paid. Their work is a strain on the eyes and a tax on the mind, and they rather dread publicity, for as soon as one of them publishes a discovery which gets into the newspapers, some ignoramus who is unworthy to loose the latchets of his shoes raises a hue and cry. So mainly they bleed within their armor and are silent, but all the time their patient work is clearing up the obscurities in translation and giving us a better and better knowledge of the Bible's exact meaning.

The other group of searchers are the literary or historical or higher critics. Who wrote these sacred books? Ezekiel claims to have written his own, and Baruch is declared to have been Jeremiah's scribe. We may infer that most of the books of the prophets were written by the men whose names they bear. But all the rest of the Old Testment is anonymous. People have rushed in to declare that certain books were written by certain men, and most of their guessing is sheer conjecture. The only way to find out who wrote a particular book, or at what time, is by a study of the book itself. For instance, when we read the first verses of Luke and find that they were written to a man named Theophilus, and then read the opening verses of Acts and find that they also are addressed to a man of the same name and that they refer to a "former treatise," we at once ask ourselves whether the two books were not written by the same man. It is a reasonable and proper question. In one way it makes no difference who wrote Luke and Acts, and if they were written by different men the fact is not of vast importance, yet both books are of more value to us when we find that the same man did write both and that the parts of Acts which use the pronoun "we" are parts which tell of events which Luke himself saw.

So it is the function of the higher critics to find out so far as they can the date and authorship and relations of the books each to the other. These critics pay little attention to other treatises; their study is the Bible itself, and in the main they are a most reverent body of men. Perhaps a few of them grow cock-sure, like young students of medicine in a dissecting room, and some of them make wrong guesses. But the only way to correct those bad guesses is by free discussion on the part of those who have special training and then by the simple criticism of common sense.

The Biblical critic to whom the world owes most is Jerome, who lived in the fourth century. By that time Latin had come to be the language of the western church and there were Latin translations of the Bible, but poor ones, made from very faulty manuscripts. Jerome was an eminent scholar, and to become still more proficient he went to Palestine and lived for a long time in Bethlehem. Two good women, a mother and her daughter, went with him; the mother, being a widow and possessed of wealth, furnished money and looked after his health. You can imagine what the pious gossips said about that arrangement. But Jerome kept on. And so did the two women. Their reputations suffered but they probably saved Jerome's life to complete its great work. He took the oldest Hebrew and Greek manuscripts he could find; he made himself a thorough master of both languages, and after years and years of lonely toil he gave the Church the Vulgate, the translation of the Bible into the "vulgar" or Latin tongue. It is the translation which the Roman Catholic Church uses to-day, and it is a noble production.

Was he thanked for his work? On the contrary, he was denounced for tampering with the word of God. His name was a byword and a reproach. But Jerome did not suffer in silence. He hit back at his critics, telling them exactly what they were. He called them "fools" and

"stupids" and "ignoramuses" and "biped asses."
To the end of his life he was cursed and denounced and called an atheist and a heretic and
a whore-monger. Meantime, by its sheer ex-
cellence his work was gaining readers in every
generation. He had to wait a thousand years
for his complete vindication—when the Council
of Trent accepted his translation as authorita-
tive. To-day we say "Saint Jerome," but he was
not called that while he was alive.

So the Bible passed into Latin and finally
into English. There had been partial translations from the Latin from the time of the Venerable Bede and King Alfred, but the name of
the great English pioneer translator is John
Wiclif, who lived from 1324 to 1384. As a
translation his work was of secondary value, for
he, too, used the Latin and not the original
tongues, but he put the Bible into the hands of
the reading public of England, which was small
but potent, and made it what it is to-day, the
Book of the common people.

One hundred and fifty years after Wiclif
came William Tyndale, who undertook a translation of the New Testament from the original
Greek. People were horror-stricken by the
impiety of the idea. He had to flee to Hamburg,
and never again set foot on his native shore.

HOW DID WE GET THE BIBLE?

Against fierce opposition he continued his work. Printing had been invented, and Tyndale determined to "make every plow-boy in England know the New Testament." His book, printed by Caxton, had to be smuggled into England and was read by stealth. With such asinine drivel as the following, written by the pious Friar Buckingham, its circulation was obstructed:

> Where Scriptures saith, "No man that layeth his hand to the plow and looketh back is fit for the kingdom of God"; will not the plowman when he readeth these words be apt forthwith to cease from his plow, and then where will be the sowing and the harvest? Likewise also whereas the baker readeth, "A little leaven leaveneth the whole lump," will he not be forthwith too sparing in the use of leaven, to the great injury of our health? And so also when the simple man reads the words, "If thine eye offend thee, pluck it out and cast it from thee," incontinent he will pluck out his eyes, and so the whole realm will be full of blind men, to the great decay of the nation and the manifest loss of the king's grace. And thus by reading of the holy Scriptures will the whole realm come into confusion.

Tyndale himself was treacherously dealt with and arrested, and lay for eighteen months in Antwerp for no crime other than that of giving to the people a truer version of the Scriptures.

On October 6, 1536, he was strangled and his body was burned. Thus have Christian folk welcomed the better and more accurate translations of the Book which teaches kindness, tolerance, forbearance and the open mind; thus do they still denounce those men of learning who would lessen their precious and sedulously guarded ignorance.

King James I of England and VI of Scotland saw that he could not prevent the reading of the Bible by the people, and he determined to get credit for what his scholars told him was much needed, a reliable translation into good English, for all the previous versions had been made under conditions that rendered exact scholarly treatment impossible. So he appointed forty-seven scholars, high church men and Puritans and those who were of no ecclesiastical party, to make a new version. Some of them had special skill in Hebrew and Greek; some were able to bring help from their knowledge of translations in the Italian, German, French and Spanish. After four years of work they gave to the world that classic, that "well of pure English, undefiled," the King James Version.

Perhaps no version in the English language will ever equal in rhythmic beauty that of the King James Version of 1671, but it is right that other versions and even new translations should be made. Each of these makes a contribution toward our better knowledge of the original. In 1885 the Revised Version was made by a joint commission of English and American scholars. Reference will be made in the next chapter to the wide interest in and influence of this scholarly version. It was agreed that the American members of the commission should issue no version of their own for fourteen years. In 1901 appeared the American Standard Revised Bible, which is, at this date, the best available text in English. Other and worthy versions continue to appear, as those of Moffatt, Goodspeed and the Riverside Bible translated by Professor William G. Ballantine. Probably no one of these will presently supersede the King James Version, but each has its value for comparison. While no important doctrine has at any time depended on any of these translations, it is proper that the very best and most scholarly minds should be engaged, as they are, in the effort to secure the nearest possible approach to a perfect text and perfect translation of the Bible into English. The two critical sciences which deal with Bible study are said, with reason, to have called forth the most severe discipline to which the human mind has ever been subjected in critical study.

THE BOOK NOBODY KNOWS

There may be readers of these pages who expected an affirmation that God in some supernatural way showed men just which books to select, dictating through all the ages the exact language of the original and teaching how to translate it free from error. It is a pity to disappoint them, but that is not the way it happened. The Bible rose to the place it now occupies because it deserved to rise to that place, and not because God sent anybody with a box of tricks to prove its divine authority. Its answer to men's spiritual needs made it what it is. Like the blacksmith's anvil that had worn out a hundred hammers and still stood firm, it has outworn the attacks of ten thousand enemies. What is more significant, it has lived in spite of the folly of its defenders.

VIII
THE INFLUENCE OF THE BOOK

TEN QUESTIONS FOR THE CURIOUS

1. *How many books, chapters, verses and words in the Old Testament? In the New Testament? In the whole Bible?*

    In King James' Version there are thirty-nine books in the Old Testament, twenty-seven in the New Testament, and sixty-six in the whole Bible. The Old Testament has 929 chapters, 31,173 verses, 693,493 words. The New Testament has 260 chapters, 7,059 verses, 181,253 words. The entire Bible has 1,189 chapters, 38,232 verses, 874,746 words. If your curiosity takes you farther than this, the Old Testament has 2,728,100 letters, the New Testament 838,380, and the entire Bible, 3,566,480.

2. *How many books, chapters, verses, and words in the Apocrypha?*

    Fourteen books, 184 chapters, 6,031 verses, 25,135 words.

3. *What is the middle book in the Old Testament? In the New? In the Bible?*

    Proverbs in the Old Testament; II Thessalonians in the New; Micah in the Bible.

4. *What is the middle chapter of the Old Testament? Of the New?*

    Job 29 of the Old Testament; Romans 13 and 14 of the New.

5. *What are the middle verses of the Old Testament? Of the New?*
   II Chronicles 20 of the Old Testament, between verses 17 and 18; Acts 17:17 of the New Testament.
6. *What is the largest book, the longest chapter in the Bible?*
   Psalms is the longest book, Psalm 119 is the longest chapter.
7. *What arc the shortest books in the Bible?*
   Obadiah in the Old Testament, Second Epistle of John in the New.
8. *What are the shortest verses in the Bible?*
   I Chronicles 1:25 in the Old Testament, John 11:35 in the New.
9. *What is the middle verse of the Bible?*
   If you are reading the Bible through by course, you will know that you are half through when you reach Psalm 18:8. The middle chapter is also the shortest chapter, Psalm 117.
10. *What verse contains the entire twenty-six letters of the English alphabet?*
    Ezra 7:21.

VIII

THE INFLUENCE OF THE BOOK

THE longest telegraphic message that ever had gone over the wires up to that time was sent from New York to Chicago, May 20, 1881. Its one hundred and eighty thousand words were addressed to *The Chicago Times,* and *The Tribune* had a message almost as long. The following morning both papers printed the four Gospels complete, with the book of Acts, while *The Times* had Romans also. The next day they printed the rest of the New Testament from copies sent by mail, proclaiming that they had performed the greatest journalistic achievement of all time. They were right. The typesetting machine was not yet in use. *The Tribune* employed ninety-two compositors and five correctors, and completed the work of taking, transcribing, correcting and setting up the text in twelve hours.

On the same day this Revised Version of the New Testament was put on sale simultaneously in New York and London. In New York

thirty-three thousand copies were sold locally
and at retail in twenty-four hours. Two million
copies were sold in Oxford and Cambridge before the edition was off the press. In the United
States, from May twentieth until the end of the
year 1881, thirty huge editions, mounting into
millions of copies, were sold. Nothing compar-
able has ever occurred in publishing history.

The New Testament has four short biographies of Jesus, each containing some material
which is not in any of the others. It has often
been asked, "Since we have four, why not more?"
Several of the apostles are supposed to have
journeyed far and to have made converts in distant places. There is nothing inherently improbable in the thought that one or more of them
might have written for his own converts in a
distant region a little sketch of Jesus as he remembered Him, and that this sketch, however
inferior as a whole to any one of our four
gospels, might contain a few authentic incidents,
one or two parables, or a report of some discourse
with Jesus hitherto unknown. It has been conjectured that such books were in actual existence.
Such conjectures are probably without foundation. But suppose that such a book, a gospel
by Thomas or Andrew, were to be found in a
far corner of Asia or Africa, and that some

scholar of a reputation as well established as that of Tischendorf, the discoverer of the Sinaitic manuscript, were to see it and pronounce it genuine. Suppose the authorities of the library or convent where it was found should say that scholars were free to examine and photograph and translate it, but that it must not be removed. What would happen?

The newspapers of New York and London, of Paris and Berlin, to say nothing of the universities in those and other countries, would charter ships to rush scholars and photographers and telegraphers to that place; they would run telegraphic lines and establish radio stations at the top of Mount Ararat or the heart of the desert of Sahara. As fast as the book could be photographed and translated, it would be printed on the front page of every newspaper in the world and broadcast from the principal radio stations. It would appear in book form almost overnight, and would outsell all the best sellers.

In the eighteenth century, that vitriolic genius, Voltaire, spoke of the Bible as a short-lived book:

The Scripture was his jest-book, whence he drew
Bon mots to gall the Christian and the Jew.

He said that within a hundred years it would pass from common use. Not many people read

THE INFLUENCE OF THE BOOK

Voltaire to-day, but his house has been packed with Bibles as the depot of a Bible society.

Thomas Paine, a much abused man, said some good things which ought to be remembered to his credit, but in closing the first part of his *Age of Reason* he left this foolish summary of what he thought he had accomplished:

> I have now gone through the Bible, as a man would go through a wood with an axe, and felled trees. Here they lie, and the priests may replant them, but they will never make them grow.

Desperate efforts have been made to replant Paine's writings and give them again the influence which they were supposed once to have had. But if the Bible sells one single copy less for anything that Paine ever wrote about or against it, the sales reports do not show it.

If a modern American author writes a book which has a moderately good sale in this country, and a London publisher takes over an edition and sells it in England, the author thinks well of his effort. If his book is translated into German or French or Spanish or Italian or Russian or Scandinavian, he has reason to be proud. He is not likely to do more than this, and he may well congratulate himself if his novel or text-book or scientific treatise appears in a half-dozen tongues. But the Bible is extant in full, from the first verse of Genesis to the end of Revelation, in one hundred and eight languages. Many other languages and dialects do not justify as yet the entire translation. New alphabets had to be made; fonts of type had to be cast; difficult sounds had to be classified; grammars and dictionaries had to be prepared, so as yet in many dialects and mixed languages only the New Testament and some portions of the Old are printed. But altogether the languages and dialects in which the Bible, either in whole or in substantial part, is in the hands of the people number about five hundred, with a billion possible readers.

How difficult this rendering of the Scriptures into strange tongues has been may be illustrated by some of the odd printings in our language. We have the "breeches" Bible, in which the aprons of Adam and Eve are thus translated; the "treacle" Bible in which "Is there no balm in Gilead?" is translated "is there no treacle, (or molasses) in Gilead?"; the "bug" Bible, with an infelicitous rendering of "creeping things," and the "wicked" Bible, with the important word "not" omitted from the seventh commandment. If, with the finest scholarship and the utmost care, such infelicities have occurred in our own

tongue, imagine the obstacles to a clear understanding of the gospel message in heathen tribes
where the language itself had to be reduced to
writing by the missionaries before the work of
translation could begin.

The man who invented the term "agnostic"
was Thomas H. Huxley, the scientist. He did
not deny, he merely did not profess to know. As
in the early Christian centuries there were certain sects that professed knowledge and called
themselves "Gnostics," he, admitting ignorance,
called himself an "Agnostic." He was a member of the London school board, and the question
was raised concerning the use of the Bible in the
schools. It was generally supposed that he
would oppose it. In *The Contemporary Review*
for December, 1871, he said:

I have always been strongly in favor of secular
education, in the sense of education without
theology, but I must confess I have been no less
seriously perplexed to know by what practical
measures the religious feeling, which is the essential
basis of conduct, was to be kept up in the present utterly chaotic state of opinion on these matters without the use of the Bible. The pagan
moralists lack life and color, and even the noble
Stoic, Marcus Antonius, is too high and refined
for an ordinary child.

Take the Bible as a whole, make the severest de-
ductions which fair criticism can dictate for

shortcomings and positive errors, as a sensible lay teacher would do if left to himself, all that is not desirable for children to occupy themselves with, and there still remains in this old literature a vast residuum of moral beauty and grandeur. And then consider the great historical fact, that for three centuries this book has been woven into the life of all that is best and noblest in English history; that it has become the national epic of Britain, and is familiar to noble and simple from John o' Groat's House to Land's End, as Dante and Tasso were once to the Italians; that it is written in the noblest and purest English, and abounds in exquisite beauties of a merely literary form; and finally, that it forbids the veriest hind who never left his village to be ignorant of the existence of other countries and other civilizations, stretching back to the furthest limits of the oldest nations in the world.

By the study of what other book could children be so much humanized, and made to feel that each figure in that vast historical procession fills, like themselves, but a momentary space in the interval between two eternities, and earns the blessings or the curses of all times, according to its efforts to do good and hate evil, even as they also are earning their payment for their work?

Professor Huxley did not stand alone in this opinion. James Anthony Froude, never accused of prejudice in favor of orthodoxy, said:

The Bible, thoroughly known, is a literature in itself—the rarest and richest in all departments of thought and imagination which exists.

300

THE INFLUENCE OF THE BOOK

Said Frederic Harrison, foremost exponent of the religion of Positivism:

> The English Bible is the true school of English literature. It possesses every quality of our language in its highest form. The book which begot English prose is still its supreme type.

Lord Macaulay wrote:

> The English Bible—a book which, if everything else in our language should perish, would alone show the whole extent of its power and beauty.

And Charles Dickens, writing to his son:

> I put a New Testament among your books for the very same reason and with the very same hopes that made me write an easy account of it when you were a little child—because it is the best book that ever was or ever will be in the world, and because it teaches you the best lessons by which any human creature who tries to be truthful and faithful can possibly be guided.

So we might discuss the Book in its influence on literature and on law; in its contribution to the spread of the English language; in its inspiration of philanthropies, for, as Lecky said in his *History of European Morals,* it has "covered the globe with countless institutions of mercy, absolutely unknown to the pagan world."

Volumes have been written, and will be, on every phase of this subject, but we do not need them. The monuments to the Book are all about us; every department of modern civilized life bears the record of its influence.

Instead of rehearsing again these well-worn testimonies, let us close our little book with a single dramatic story, a story so old that surely many readers will find it entirely new.

It starts with George III of England, in the year 1768. In that year the Royal Society of London appealed to the King to send a royal expedition to the South Seas to observe a transit of Venus across the disk of the sun, which event was to occur in 1769. A bark of three hundred and seventy tons was accordingly sent out, and the island chosen was for a time called King George's Island, but later it became and at present is known by its native name of Otaheite, or, in its abbreviated form, Tahiti. It is there the modern writers go to get local color for their South Sea stories.

Out of this expedition to observe the transit of Venus grew another, and a most worthy undertaking it was. It had been found that certain of the islands were uninhabited or nearly so because they had no adequate food supply. It was believed that if trees of the breadfruit palm were transplanted to them these islands would become habitable, so in 1787 King George consented to the sending out of another small ship, the *Bounty*. She was of two hundred and fifteen tons burden, and had officers and crew numbering forty-four, besides two men skilled in the culture of trees. The *Bounty* sailed from Spithead, England, December 23, 1787, and arrived at Tahiti October 26, 1788, having sailed twenty-seven thousand and eighty-six miles.

Cupid is an important character in all South Sea stories. The sailors were much more interested in the native girls than they were in digging up young trees. They saw with real reluctance the ship's growing cargo, for it meant that they might have to leave their sweethearts, which they did not like to do. "For twenty-three weeks," wrote Captain Bligh, "we had been treated with the utmost affection and regard, which seemed to increase in proportion to our stay." If the men in the fo'castle had written up the log they would have said the same. But they had to leave.

The doctor had died through indolence and intemperance; but the captain records that the ship was in perfect order, the crew in excellent health, the trees all flourishing. Just before sunrise on the morning of April twenty-eight, however, a mutiny broke out, unprovoked save by the wish of the crew to return to the dusky girls. The captain and eighteen men were set adrift in an open boat, with a hundred and fifty pounds of bread, sixteen pieces of pork averaging two pounds each, six quarts of rum, six bottles of wine, and twenty-eight gallons of water.

Faced by stark necessity, all the captain's power as a disciplinarian came to the fore. He rationed his men at the minimum that would sustain life and give energy to their arms, and he set out to row three thousand six hundred miles. At night they spread their blankets to the dew and sucked them to save water, and they caught a few birds. After severe hardships they completed their incredible voyage, landed at an inhabited island, and were shipped home to England, arriving there in March, 1790.

An expedition was dispatched at once to seek out the pirates, fourteen of whom were captured and brought back. Four died in a shipwreck on the way home; four were acquitted; one was discharged through an informality in the indictment, and five were hanged. But nine of the mutineers had not remained where they could be captured. Little as they expected that the tiny boat would ever reach England, they determined to take no chances. They shipped on the

Bounty, taking with them six native men, ten women and a girl of fifteen, and sailed away to an island named Pitcairn, after the British officer who fired the first shot at Lexington.

Then ensued what the *Encyclopedia Britannica* calls "a hell on earth." One of the sailors had worked in a distillery in Scotland and he discovered a way to distil alcohol from a native plant. Before a great while all the native men were dead, and all the white men but one. That one was Alexander Smith, left alone with a harem of native women and a crowd of half-breed children, his own and his companions'.

Picture him, if you will, the forlorn monarch of a helpless people, shut up with his own bitter memories. Then consider the thing which happened. In one of the chests of the sailors he found a book. He read it. He began to ask himself what was to become of this population that had had such a bad start. He began to think with shame and remorse of all the past; he repented of his sins and resolved to live a God-fearing life, and to make good men and women of those children. He began to teach those children to read that book. So years passed. The children grew up and married, and more children were born. The community prospered.

Then one day, nearly twenty years later, in

1808, the United States ship *Topaz* called at this island and brought back the first word which the world had received of the mutineers who escaped the hangman in 1790. Alexander Smith was king and preacher and teacher in that little community. In honor of the President of the United States he had changed his name to John Adams, and he much hoped that only ships from America would visit him, for he had no hankering for the gallows in England. But no British expedition went out after him, and he lived and died in peace.

And now, what about the people on that island?

There was no jail.

There was no hospital.

There was no insane asylum.

There was no illiteracy, no crime, no disease.

The people had no doctors, took no medicine, used no liquor.

The island was one hundred per cent. Christian; nowhere on earth were life and property more safe.

What changed that place from a hell on earth to a little speck of heaven dropped down in the South Seas?

The reading of The Book.

THE END